You'll Miss Me When I'm Gone

A Celebration of the Life and Work of Eric Morecambe

GARY MORECAMBE

HarperCollins*Publishers*

HarperCollins*Publishers*
77–85 Fulham Palace Road,
Hammersmith, London W6 8JB
www.harpercollins.co.uk

First published by HarperCollins*Publishers* 2009

1 3 5 7 9 10 8 6 4 2

Gary Morecambe asserts the moral right
to be identified as the author of this work

A catalogue record of this book is
available from the British Library

ISBN 978-0-00-728732-1

Printed and bound in China by
Leo Paper Products Limited

All photographs courtesy of Gary Morecambe, with exception of pp 15, 16, 21 & 24 (©
Rex Features) and pp 101, 104 & 105 (© PA Photos). The author would also like to thank
Bernard Wrigley for granting permission to reproduce his poem 'Upon the occasion of the
unveiling of the plaque at no. 43 Christie Avenue'.

While every effort has been made to trace the owners of copyright material reproduced
herein, the publishers would like to apologise for any omissions and will be pleased to
incorporate missing acknowledgements in any future editions.

For my mother, Joan,
because I've never taken the time
to say thank you for everything.

In memory of my friend and former colleague
Eddie Waters who died suddenly this year.

'I remain one thing and one thing only, and that is a clown. It places me on a far higher plane than any politician.' CHARLIE CHAPLIN

'It takes courage and openness to achieve authenticity — to be able to say to yourself and to the world, "Like it or not, this is who I am," and then to live that truth.' DAN MILLMAN

'[Morecambe and Wise are] the greatest double act in the history of British television.' THE INDEPENDENT

Contents

Foreword

by Dame Judi Dench OBE

Like everybody else, I was completed bewitched by *The Morecambe and Wise Show*. It was the highlight of the week to watch and never to be missed. When the glorious moment came of being invited to appear on the show, I could not wait. I was SO excited! Among other things, we did Ernie's version of *Dr Jekyll and Mr Hyde*. I remember Eric walking through the set of a foggy London with three legs! We laughed until we wept. He also kept calling me 'young man'. Eric and Ernie were the most amazing complement to each other.

My late husband, the actor Michael Williams, and I saw quite a lot of Eric afterwards and he often came to our house for a meal. The first time this happened, Eric asked me what was for dinner. When I told him it was salmon, he said he would just have the vegetables, and I thought it was a joke. It turned out that he really did not like salmon and did just eat the vegetables. The next time, he brought with him a whole salmon that he had caught himself – and still just had the vegetables!

Eric was genuinely funny, but never unkind with his humour. I still miss him and shall never forget him. This book, commemorating the twenty-fifth anniversary of Eric's passing, is the most wonderful tribute to an extraordinary man.

DAME JUDI DENCH OBE

Letter

from Ronnie Corbett OBE

Dear Gary,

Of course I knew Eric very well indeed. We were both members of the Lord's Taverners at the same time, and of course saw each other quite a lot at their functions, and their dinners and their balls etc., and Joan and he were always a delight to bump into, and Joan remains so of course.

I probably didn't know Eric nearly as well as Ronnie B did, because I have been a South London boy, although I'm a Scotsman of course, but I have lived in South London all my life. Ronnie lived always up in the Hatch End area, and Eric also living North of London saw somewhat more of him I think; they even had dinners together at their homes, so Ron was more of an expert than me on him, but of course I am a huge admirer of Eric.

He still remains, doesn't he, in anything you read, top of the list at a time when comics were great, dear, clean and very funny, like Tommy Cooper, and Ken Dodd remains to this day. So Ronnie and I were existing in a very keenly expert world.

We were in no way competitive, because we were quite different. Eric and Ernie grew up together, they developed together. I think they may have known each other from being 14 or 15, whereas Ron and I didn't really come together until we were about 37, so there was not a spiritual coming together in the same way, which was an important difference, and a very classic fact.

Ron and I were brought together as two single artists, who got on well and worked very, very comfortably together, and enjoyed it tremendously, but we weren't joined in the same way emotionally from teenage years as Eric and Ernie were, and I think it probably *made for the crucial difference in our styles. Ron and I were both great admirers of Eric and Ernie. We often rehearsed in the same building, the Acton Hilton, and used to bump into each other now and again there. We rehearsed at different times, but we tended to start a bit earlier in the day I think, and they went on a little bit later, and if I remember correctly, we drove ourselves, and Eric and Ernie were very often chauffeured. A mild distinction I daresay.*

As far as being socially funny, Eric was wondrous. In company he was absolutely sparklingly contemporarily original. He couldn't help himself in a way, and I often wondered if there was a strain which eventually took its toll.

He wasn't one, I do remember, to stand up and say much on his own, because of course he did miss Ernie if they weren't together, because he felt he had someone to lean on, or someone to refer to, so he wasn't that sort of animal, but as you sat at a dinner table, or mingled with a few drinks before dinner, he sparkled, and he was the most winning of people in company.

I can't say more really. It's fantastic that they still remain at the top of any journalist's list of funny people now and in days gone by. God bless him.

Ronnie Corbett OBE
12 June 2008

Remembering Eric

This Boy's a Fool

INTERVIEWER: *Some say you never mix socially. Is this true?*

ERIC: *It is true, and it isn't true. The point is, if we have to mix socially we will. If we don't, we don't. That's what has helped to keep us together such a long time.*

ERNIE: *People seem to think the image extends from the stage … like Laurel and Hardy.*

This almost certainly being the last book I will ever write on my father, Eric Morecambe, I want to put down a few words about the man from a personal standpoint.

A family Sunday lunch conversation was taking place in the Morecambe household circa 1970. We were discussing, in far from dulcet tones, as was the way when my father was about, various ideas he had for his next Christmas show. Not unnaturally we were all eager to chip in with our own ideas. Finally, beneath the hum of voices, my father, in his familiarly loud tones said, 'Be quiet, everyone. Gary's got something to say, and every now and then it can be interesting!'

I cannot recall for the life of me what I then suggested that long-ago day, but hopefully this book – commemorating the twenty-fifth anniversary of the great man's passing – is the 'now and then' when I can be interesting.

Some observers of past books to do with family relationships where fame is

Author with Eric in 1982. This photo was taken by Eric's publicist, and the author's friend, Eddie Waters. It was taken before their joint publicity tour to promote the author's first book on his father, Funny Man.

present, including one publication of my own, appear to misunderstand the whole concept of consigning to print the personal experiences and events of their life around that fame. Friend and erstwhile colleague, the late Michael Sellers, son of one of my own personal heroes, Peter Sellers, wrote a very compelling biography of his father in the early eighties called *PS: I Love You*. At the time he was put under a lot of pressure for having made 'slanderous' comments about his father and generally trawling for dirt – neither of which he did! He simply told the story in a very honest and balanced way. The misconception, therefore, is that the author is always out to trawl for dirt and not simply aiming to define the image of the parent of public interest as they, the author, experienced it.

Therefore, whatever you might read into my words, rest assured of one thing: Eric Morecambe is still my icon and the best father anyone could wish to have had.

Fortunately there is a big difference between Eric Morecambe and Peter Sellers when it comes to personalities, and I'm so very lucky that out of all the famous parents I might have had I got Eric! And it's not whingeing or dirt-trawling when I try to give the complete image of the man. It is providing an accurate account (as accurate as one person's experiences and observations ever can be trusted to be) not only for his fans of today but also for those of future years.

As I say, I'm lucky because Eric was a thoroughly pleasant person to be around, who, in his own words, 'never knowingly set out to hurt anyone'. His shortcomings and doubts as a parent were more to do with the extraordinary circumstances of his chosen career and the fact that that career made him absent quite a bit, specifically in my sister's and my early years. Furthermore, it was an era when fathers were heard more than seen. In his case he wasn't heard that much either, because most of the parenting was left to my mother, owing mostly to those protracted absences. This must have made it difficult for him — and her, come to think of it. Yet he did manage to connect with us so well. The comedy performer's thing of touching the child within certainly is true: as soon as he was around there was little time wasted growing accustomed to who this man we called 'Dad' was. All at once he was just there, and joking around and communicating on our level.

'Eric was a thoroughly pleasant person to be around, who, in his own words, "never knowingly set out to hurt anyone".'

Occasionally he would act more seriously and there'd be the 'How's school going?' question. I liked those questions, not because he was genuinely interested, because he wasn't — it was an alien world for him and the wash of blankness over his face showed as much — but because he felt he *should* ask, and that was heartfelt and therefore warmly received.

I reflect on him as a performer who was absorbed by his work – a performer who saw his career as much more than a means to an end. This was probably detrimental to his health, but not to the extent claimed by certain documentaries, which casually gloss over the sixty fags a day and the ill-health he acquired working down the mines. But it is fair to state that his personality was not fully geared to the pressures that being on top of the comedy pile had in store. He

often claimed that being something just a little less than number one was best, because you had a great living without carrying the stress of public expectation. Having been in his company in public I would challenge that, as I got the impression that he very much enjoyed being number one. He certainly enjoyed being famous: a documentary by Jonathan Ross screened at Christmas 2007 confirmed as much when in a rare interview from the archives my father admitted to it without a moment's hesitation. In fact, he went on to say that he didn't believe other famous people when they said that they *didn't* enjoy it.

I also sense with my father that he saw his success as a stroke of luck – something that prevented him having to do an underpaid, mundane job for a living. I don't think I heard him ever knock his father, George, for spending a life working for the Corporation (local council), but equally he felt no urge to follow in his footsteps.

'Fundamentally he just wanted to make us, his family, laugh and make the viewing public laugh too.'

I think, as we'll see from the words of his old friends from Lancashire, that Eric was a little unusual as a child: clearly gifted, yet sometimes remote when he chose to be. All these friends seemed to expect him to go on to great things as if it were a given. His sharp wit, inability to deal with responsibilities and major decisions, and a temperament which made it difficult for him to be tolerant of all that everyday life threw his way would all have been a part of him with or without the recognition and success that followed. However, I would say that the nature of his work added to any stress he felt and contributed to his momentary mood swings. But, as I write these words, I know that fundamentally he just wanted to make us, his family, laugh and make the viewing public laugh too. He was somehow beholden to that need to entertain because it had freed him from an ordinary background, yet in the act of embracing it he

became imprisoned by it. That's really all it came down to. All the other bits were just flighty little moments of everyday life – some days were good and fun and full of hilarity around the house, some days less so. All other expressions, desires and actions were hardly recognizable as anything more than minor character traits: there really wasn't that much there beyond entertaining – it totally defined him and was virtually all he was seeking from life.

What helped damage his health was the incongruity that being funny was not – and probably isn't for *any* comedian – delivered from a relaxed state of mind and body. As my mother once remarked, he could hardly sit down at the dinner table without having to get up and do something halfway through the meal. He was a bundle of nervous energy. This made him slightly contradictory, for while Morecambe and Wise was everything to him, he was also quite happy to point out clouds and make shapes from them, or to sit alone all day long on the river bank, surrendering to the moment and revelling in that childlike clarity of vision that was so much a part of his likeability.

People often approach me and say, 'You look just like your dad.' This I find very uplifting and flattering, for my brush-over grey-white hair makes me look much more like Ernie these days. Even friends and family remark about the similarity – to my father, that is, not Ernie. It's also friends and family who express a quiet concern that I spend too much time working on Morecambe and Wise-related projects and issues, to the detriment of other things, but I'm too old to change. And although I do other projects I never tire of the Morecambe and Wise ones – indeed I would dispense with all the rest in favour of these, because first and foremost I'm as much a fan of Eric and Ernie as I am Eric's son. I still sit at home and watch the DVDs, and amaze myself that I always laugh and laugh as much as ever. Some humour really is timeless.

It is summer 2008. While the birds twitter and the bees hum, and the man next door tries drowning them out with his lawnmower, I'm sitting at my computer writing the book you are now holding. I feel unbelievably excited. It's always the same. When it's to do with Morecambe and Wise I seem to ignite. This ignition is automatic, yet still I can't resist going through all my favourite

routines of theirs for an excess of inspiration. It's probably just an excuse to watch all their shows again. With the advent of YouTube I even spend my lunch break watching them getting up to mischief with the likes of John Lennon: I love the way he throws back his head in hysterics when Eric ad-libs. Then there's André Previn and his wonderful orchestra performing Grieg's Piano Concerto with Eric as soloist; Eric and Ernie 'backing' Tom Jones; Shirley Bassey having her shoe replaced with a workman's boot; Glenda Jackson in *that* Cleopatra sketch ('Sorry I'm late, but I've been irrigating the desert ... not easy on your own!'); Eric and Ernie making breakfast to *The Stripper*; or their homage to Gene Kelly with their beautifully shot *Singin' in the Rain*. The list is endless.

It's the going back to the many magical moments of their television career that reminds me – should I need reminding – that they were absolute masters of comedy; and that they are not just for ever but also inimitable. There is something dynamic and glittering about the two of them that prevents their work from tiring – something that goes beyond the fact they were mere comic entertainers providing light relief in an otherwise tragic world. Perhaps it is a combination of their wonderful talent as performers and the lost era from which they emerged. Arguably they are the last great 'stars' Britain produced – a legend that goes way beyond today's vacuous notion of 'celebrity'.

The novelist L.P. Hartley wrote: 'The past is a foreign country: they do things differently there.' Many are the times that this observation comes to mind, and more often than not it is when I'm thinking about the heyday of Morecambe and Wise, which is basically any year in the seventies. What is it about that decade – that cringe-worthy, decadent, crudely flamboyant, sexist, gaudy, tasteless time – that allowed Morecambe and Wise to reign supreme as the kings of British comedy? This was still the era of the suit-and-tie comedian – 'alternative comedy' hadn't even been thought of, let alone given that title, and if a performer had the temerity to appear on TV minus a tie or indeed a jacket, you sensed they wouldn't be making too many more screen appearances, while simultaneously concluding they must have been dragged out of some working men's club to 'have a go' on the box. Now we can look back from today's current crop of comedy entertainers and the boot is firmly on the other foot, as we wonder: yes, Eric and Ernie were and for ever will be a remarkable comedy act, but why did they dress like second-hand-car salesmen?

'Eric is not only England's most popular comedian, he must be near to being our most popular person.'

Author-playwright-novelist-lawyer the late John Mortimer wrote in 1983: 'Eric is not only England's most popular comedian, he must be near to being our most popular person.'

Which neatly sums up why, after fifty-two years on this planet, I still celebrate my father's life and work in books such as this: frankly, there is a demand for him, and the fact that my father died suddenly mid-flow a quarter of a century ago has not remotely lessened the love for him felt by those who vividly remember the wonderful shows he and Ernie produced, and by others who are discovering them for the first time.

From Morecambe Bay to Broadway

'My most special memory of Morecambe is the day the whole town came to see me off – and told me never to come back.'

As a kid Eric could only dream of the bright lights of Broadway. That, one day in the distant future, a November night in 2001, there would be a play about his (and his partner's) life on a West End stage would have been incomprehensible.

The Play What I Wrote, in its initial concept, was an idea of mine, along with writer Martin Sterling and West End producer David Pugh. We wanted to stage a tribute to the legendary double act. It might well have remained just a drawing-board notion had it not been for The Right Size, a comedy team with a great stage track record, coming up with the ini-

From the touring production of The Play What I Wrote, *the tribute stage show to Morecambe and Wise, and which this author remembers as the happiest project on which he ever worked.*

by Hamish McColl and Sean Foley
and, of course, Eddie Braben

NEW VICTORIA THEATRE, WOKING

tiative of writing a play about their own lives in which they happen to become like Eric and Ernie as they go about performing their own tribute to them. And so a potentially good idea turned into a well-executed reality. When actor-director Kenneth Branagh agreed to direct the project, adding West End credibility to the production, the final piece of the jigsaw was in place. And if that wasn't good enough, the play was destined to transfer to New York after a staggeringly successful run at London's Wyndham's Theatre.

Ken Branagh had an early introduction to the world of Morecambe and Wise. 'When I was fourteen,' he told a journalist in 2002, 'I wrote to Morecambe and Wise to ask for tickets for one of their TV shows. The letter that came back was one of the first ever addressed to me at my house. It had BBC stamped at the top of the envelope, and as I ran downstairs to collect it, my brother, who was in particularly bullying mode at the time, was so completely intrigued, he actually opened it.

'Inside was a signed photograph. And although there were no tickets left, and I never got to see Morecambe and Wise live, I still have the photo to this day.'

Ken was fascinated by them from watching them on TV. 'I vividly remember a documentary about Morecambe and Wise,' he recalls, 'and I couldn't imagine anything more exciting than seeing what Morecambe and Wise did, and how they actually did it.'

The play was first tested at the Everyman Theatre in Liverpool. 'We did a lot of "dying" in Liverpool,' says Ken, through a wry smile. 'It wasn't right at that time. Hamish [McColl, who portrays the Ernie part of the duo] swore that the answer to making it work was to have Sean wear Eric's glasses. So for one show we did this and planned some more Eric-like business to be going on – and it was a disaster! Total disaster!

'Audiences weren't having it, even though it was one inch closer to being Eric. The audience somehow needed to see the play through a kind of prism – through someone else's physicality.

'It took the whole month in Liverpool to work out the shape for this homage; this affectionate presentation of Eric and Ernie.'

The run on the West End stage, and the wonderful list of guest stars who appeared in the show, reached a natural conclusion, but as is so often the case with Morecambe and Wise, so much seems to continue happening with them each passing year despite both having left us some time ago. Broadway is the biggest development in the history of the show.

Catching up for lunch with Ken some six years since we worked together on the project, it was wonderful to find his enthusiasm for both Morecambe and Wise and the play itself had not remotely diminished.

'In Hamish [McColl], Sean [Foley] and Toby's [Jones, who played myriad roles in the production] performances you have the perfect degree of ego and neurosis that keeps it edgy and really challenging,' he explains. 'Because Hamish and Sean as The Right Size had been together a long time with their own successful partnership prior to the production meant that they were bringing something to it which was way beyond re-creation of Morecambe and Wise. You need to have performers who come out of a similar kind of box – hard-working and talented as the act they are paying homage to.'

We discussed the first night, and all of us associated with the play were very nervy that day as tickets had gone on sale to little reaction. 'One of the things I remember about that first night in London,' says Ken, 'was the quality of the audience – all these "names" dotted around the auditorium – and feeling this huge desire for it to go well.

'When I saw Bruce Forsyth several times leaning forward doubled up with laughter, I felt so relieved. No disrespect to Bruce Forsyth, but comedians aren't normally regarded for their generosity to other comedians, so I took it as a very good omen that Bruce was clearly loving it.'

It was the first night success and subsequent reviews that brought about its almost immediate success.

But taking it to Broadway was always going to be a very different venture. Ken Branagh had some reservations about Broadway from the outset, which were echoed by me, The Right Size and Toby Jones.

'It was always going to be a challenge taking the play on to Broadway,' explains Ken, diplomatically. 'Despite a well-worked script and the comedic skills of Hamish, Sean and Toby, what it lacked in New York that it never had lacked in the UK in its West End life and various touring productions was a massive level of affection.

'In a sense, Eric and Ern hijacked Christmas, but it was the most beautiful piece of hijacking.'

'To the audiences in the UK it went way beyond finding Eric and Ernie funny; it was the whole nostalgia their memory and reputation brought to the stage production. As well as being genuinely, unmistakably on the highest level funny, Morecambe and Wise's best work coincided with moments in the life of the nation – especially Christmas – when everyone was together. Symbolically they came to represent that togetherness.

From left to right: Sean Foley, Toby Jones and Hamish McColl. Sean and Hamish – The Right Size – in mid-flow during their tribute to Eric and Ernie at the Wyndham's theatre, London. Toby played just about every other role.

Above right: **Many famous guest stars alongside Sean, Hamish and Toby, who made a collective appearance in a special charity performance. Sting, Richard Wilson, David Suchet and Charles Dance catch the eye immediately. Sting was one of my personal favourites, and he had the funniest line of the play. He says to Sean, 'I'll have you know I've appeared in over fifty films.' Sean, scratching his head, responds, 'But how many have you had developed?!'**

Above left: **Roger Moore reminiscing his role as 007 with the support of Bond 'Luvlies' Angela Rippon, Miranda Richardson (foreground) and Denise Van Outen.**

Roger Moore doing the routine which literally nearly killed him.

The iconic M&W skip-dance image. What I like about this is the ghostly background silhouettes of Eric and Ernie. The idea was from Irving Davies, the play's choreographer.

'In a sense, Eric and Ern hijacked Christmas, but it was the most beautiful piece of hijacking that meant that at that moment when the people of the nation were together they were simultaneously finding themselves associated with Morecambe and Wise's comedy.'

Opening on Broadway would be less about Morecambe and Wise and more about the camaraderie of all double acts. I understood the logic behind the decision, but was concerned that by removing the spirit of Morecambe and Wise we were removing the whole purpose of why we originally set out to stage the show.

The general feeling was that many theatregoers who came to see the West End production were American, Japanese, Chinese, and other, and they enjoyed it enormously, laughing their way out into the Covent Garden night when the curtain came down. I wasn't convinced about that: surely, I thought, its success was due to the feelgood factor of Eric and Ernie working on those mostly British members of successive audiences who remembered Christmases past? That invisible awareness was actively, if unwittingly, being sucked up by those in the audience not in the least bit familiar with Eric and Ernie or their work. In New York that would not be possible as there would be no such underlying sentiment.

I must credit David Pugh for having the balls to give it a whirl, as it was his reputation and money on the line. And – if in hugely diluted form – he did get Morecambe and Wise introduced to a much wider audience.

Decisions can be made quickly – if rashly – in the entertainment business I discovered, and in February 2003 one relatively under-utilized consultant to the US production was flown out in first-class style to join the team as the opening night loomed. My mother, Joan, was also to be there for that night, which, while it was expected, was a bit discomforting given that her husband – half the *raison d'être* of the London production – had inevitably been reduced from being the play's subject to appearing in the programme notes.

My mother and I were put up at the colourful Algonquin Hotel at 59 West 44th Street, between Fifth and Sixth Avenues, a spit from Times Square. The reason I mention this hotel with a hint of admiration is because one of my great heroes, Harpo Marx, a gentleman and a giant of visual comedy, many decades back would frequent the place to play cards with some of his mates: screen-writer Robert Benchley (father of Peter Benchley, who gave us the novel *Jaws!*) and poet, critic, and short-story writer Dorothy Parker, to name but two. They and others formed an exclusive club, the Round Table, to pursue their delight in gambling, intellectual conversation and dry wit. The only rule seemed to be that you had to be able to take the knocks – there was no room for taking offence or acting self-important. Harpo was invited to join this elite club by his good friend the critic Alexander Woollcott. As some people get excited by treading the well-worn paths that Eric Morecambe trod, I get the same thrill from being in the vicinity of where a Marx Brother stood, walked, talked, breathed, laughed, cried, and anything else they might have done, especially when it is my favourite Marx Brother, the mute and blond, curly-locked Harpo – not that he was either of those things in real life, of course. And I was doubly blessed when discovering the theatre we were opening at was the Lyric – the very same theatre the Marx Brothers had opened at with the musical *The Cocoanuts* many decades earlier.

One of the first people my mother and I stumbled across at the Algonquin was actor Roger Moore and his wife Kristina. Roger had been the stalwart guest star of the London production. I don't think any guest star made as many appearances. He even guest-starred in towns such as Milton Keynes on a wet Wednesday afternoon while the play toured for a while. A long way from his homes in Monaco and Switzerland. Although he wasn't due to appear on the opening night on Broadway – 'They don't think I'm famous enough!' he told us with his usual disarming charm – he did guest on many subsequent nights there, in between which he would fly all round the world doing his sterling work for the United Nations Children's Fund. In fact this fast and furious lifestyle was to prove a little too much for a man who was in his mid-seventies at the time. During one of the Broadway performances Roger blacked out on stage. The audience thought it was part of the show. Eventually he came round, still on stage, to find Hamish McColl (who loosely represents Ernie Wise in the play) standing above him. 'Are you all right, old boy?' asked Hamish. 'I think so, old boy,' replied Roger, who then insisted on finishing that night's performance before being transferred to hospital by the paramedics who had been summoned immediately and were waiting in the wings.

'During one of the Broadway performances Roger blacked out on stage. The audience thought it was part of the show.'

It was at this point in that particular Roger Moore story that on a visit to London I began my conversation with Hamish McColl, the actor and co-writer of the play, and co-founder of The Right Size. We quickly realized it had been nearly five years since we last got together, and that had been in New York.

Hamish, who is currently not acting but writing – he wrote the hugely successful movie *Mr Bean's Holiday* for Rowan Atkinson – started out by recalling that event which shocked us all and was big news in the tabloid press in Britain.

'There were so many highs in that play,' said Hamish, 'but the biggest low was definitely when Roger collapsed right next to us on stage. It was frightening because he dropped like a tree being felled. He hit the ground and didn't move. We were terrified. We thought he was dead. It was one of those moments when I couldn't think of any bright improvisation line, so just started waving my arms around and shouting out "close the curtains". He's an absolute trooper. He sat up and insisted on finishing the performance, then went off to hospital to have his pacemaker fitted. Two days later he was attending a big function for UNICEF.'

Eric and Ernie came to use their childhood training in dancing with more frequency in the 1970s Morecambe and Wise show when under the guidance of choreographer (and later producer) Ernest Maxin. Eric and Ernie had talked for some while about bringing a more Hollywood musical flavour to their productions, and they always saw Ernest as the man to deliver this mutual love of song and dance.

And the next night of the play after Roger had been taken away sick?

'Alan Alda, most famous for his role in *M.A.S.H.*, stepped in and was brilliant,' explained Hamish. 'What made it work so well with him was the fact that his parents had been vaudevillians. He would watch the first half of the show from the wings, and I think he was the only guest star who did that. Normally they just made their entrance in the second half.'

Apparently Roger's daughter, Deborah, had told Hamish that her father was terrified of doing the play. Also, Hamish said, 'Ken [Branagh] told me when we were still at the rehearsal stage that the higher the status of the star the more terrified they will be. That was a very good tip. Roger played it pretty much like he was Prince Rainier of Monaco, when he first arrived. It was the blazer and dark glasses and not very communicative approach. Of course you could misread this and think that he was being deliberately aloof, but it transpired that he was just terrified about appearing in the play. When we got to know him he could not have been nicer. He was charming; he went on to do the show countless times both in the UK and the States, his wife always accompanying him. Wonderful. And I also went out to Switzerland and saw them there and was made very welcome.'

It was fascinating to hear Hamish's own thoughts on something to which he was integral in making it such a huge success. Our previous times together had been while the play was up and running, so until now we hadn't had the opportunity for this dispassionate 'with hindsight' overview of what that remarkably exciting period for all of us involved had been about. And, as consultant to the production, my role was firstly to nit-pick the script and later their performances in respect of their adopting, and consistently sustaining, the Morecambe and Wise feel in their delivery and actions. Obviously what was needed of me was to bring to the production any knowledge that being Eric Morecambe's son and self-acclaimed know-all and walking A–Z on Morecambe and Wise gave me. This was essentially the role I had planned for myself back in the mid-nineties when first discussing the project with David Pugh.

The play would continue for several years right up to April 2007, but by then without its creators and performers Hamish McColl and Sean Foley. And what a list of guest stars had during that time graced their production: Ioan Gruffudd, Denise Van Outen, Charles Dance, George Cole, Simon Callow, Nigel Havers, Sue Johnston, Dawn French, Michael Starke, Ralph Fiennes, Richard E. Grant, Sting, Bob Geldof, Roger Moore, Kylie Minogue, Cilla Black, Maureen Lipman, Richard Wilson, David Suchet, Ewan McGregor — and they're just the ones that readily spring to mind. Madonna came to see it, as did Pierce Brosnan, and both showed positive interest. But time passed quickly and before the availability of either could be confirmed, Sean and Hamish's production was over.

My mother, Shaun Prendergast and me at a Comic Heritage function. Shaun – who until recently was in Emmerdale – was originally working on the idea of the M&W play with me and erstwhile writer (and Corrie writer) Martin Sterling prior to David Pugh doing his own production.

'I can't watch any of the new productions of it,' Hamish admits with a hint of melancholy. 'Not after my involvement. The strangest thing of all was preparing the scripts for the first new cast. There came that point where I had to press the button which erased all our names – Me, Sean and Toby [Jones] – and replace them with the new cast. We were gone!'

I can't help agreeing with Hamish when he says, 'My personal feeling is that it could have run another year in the West End, it was such a big success and an award-winner. But it's always something we could bring back to the West End in due course.'

The idea of the play making a return in its original form with the original team is an intriguing one considering that Hamish and Sean had gone their separate ways after a remarkable seventeen years together. 'Not nearly as long as Eric and Ernie were together,' Hamish said, 'but still a considerable time.' Was this a consequence of doing the play together? I wondered.

'Not at all,' Hamish was quick to point out. 'We both had other things we wanted to try out. It was just time for change. And as I say, we would reunite for *The Play What I Wrote,* should that opportunity resurface.'

Hamish shares my misgivings about taking what was primarily a play about the spirit of Morecambe and Wise over to New York, where they were hardly known.

'You say they are the spirit of the play; I would go further and say the entire soul of it,' he said. 'It became a different show. It became a show about a double act in crisis and their need to stay together, but it didn't have that crucial emotional resonance that it had in the purely Eric and Ernie version in Britain. And you underestimate those things at your peril. Morecambe and Wise were the blood-line of the piece, and it made it much more difficult for us in America. We still got a lot of laughs, and good audiences showed up – we were never below half-full – but you sensed that vital connection to the audience was missing.

'That was the magic thing about Eric and Ernie that made us want to do the play in the first place. Actually,' he corrected himself, 'it was what made us *not* want to do it at the outset. I mean, how can you go out and imitate an icon act like Morecambe and Wise? Until we found that device of it being about *us* as a way to do *them*, it wasn't feasible.'

I can relate to this, of course, as I'd spent several years having the same discussions with David Pugh. Quickly we recognized that a pure imitation was not a possible way to execute the idea of a tribute to Morecambe and Wise.

After the low moment with Roger being taken to hospital halfway through a Broadway performance, what was for Hamish the high moment of the months spent in the West End, then on Broadway, and later on tour in the UK?

'I have many,' he said with a warm smile. 'If we're talking guest stars, and there were very, very few who didn't really cut the mustard, then I suppose that you can name them on the basis of audience reaction. Firstly, we had Toby always on the side of the stage doing an impression of the guest star that then quietly walks on to the stage from the other wing. Some got muted applause, some good applause and some huge applause. But if they were a massive name, then you got a momentary pause during which the audience is thinking, can this really be them? Roger Moore was in this last category and also Sting, Kylie Minogue, Ewan McGregor, and Richard E. Grant. Richard did the show lots of times, a bit like Roger. John McEnroe, of course, in the New York production, was massive. He just got it totally. You had Toby Jones at one end of the stage and John McEnroe at the other shouting out in New York whines: 'No, *I'm* John McEnroe.' 'No you're not – *I'm* John McEnroe.' Brilliant. Those names named are some of the big highs of the two runs and the short tour we did with the play. There were times in that show I would turn to Sean and say, "Listen to that laughter because you'll never hear it as thick again." That play really was a laughter machine. It was like being at a rock concert, not a stage play!'

'There were times in that show I would turn to Sean and say, "Listen to that laughter because you'll never hear it as thick again".'

After the play finished, Hamish and Sean did not immediately part company to pursue independent challenges. Quite quickly they went into a new stage production which reunited the whole *The Play What I Wrote* team of Hamish McColl, Sean Foley, Toby Jones, Kenneth Branagh (as director), and David Pugh (as producer). This was to be the maligned and ill-fated *Ducktastic!*

The main reason it failed, in this humble writer's opinion, is because the title is truly dire. For my money, any play named *Ducktastic!* sounds more like something the Krankies would come up with. Remember them? Fandabidozi! It must, therefore, have been an uphill battle from the opening onwards – and there wasn't too much 'onwards'!

But Hamish McColl has his own theories. 'I think we set the bar too high with *The Play What I Wrote*. The next production just didn't catch on,' he explained. 'It was an expensive show to stage, and they didn't have the time to bridge that gap between an average start and developing it into something a bit special. So it was pulled.'

My mind drifts back to the opening night of *The Play What I Wrote*, *before* Roger was ill, *before* Hamish and Sean misfired with *Ducktastic!*, and *before* the lovely and talented Toby Jones began scaling the heights as the big star he deserved to become (he won stunning reviews for his depiction of Truman Capote): this was the opening night of *The Play What I Wrote* on Broadway and it was clearly very successful with the audience, if a little confusing for the family, friends, and fans of Morecambe and Wise. At one point the names of More-cambe and Wise are replaced with those of Laurel and Hardy. Inevitably it was only what it could ever be: a goodish play well performed with a famous guest star each night. Maybe that would have been enough for Broadway if there had been no 9/11 and no war on Iraq.

The first-night party was a very New York affair – lots of money lavished upon a vast number of guests in a huge first-floor room just off Times Square – and you sensed the party meant more to the American side of the production than their British counterparts. There were paparazzi-style columns of pho-tographers and TV news crews, and unbearably bright lights and loud, chat-tering voices trying to be heard through fixed Botox grins. As David Pugh pointed out, he would rather have seen the thousands of dollars they splashed out on partying go towards publicity. But that isn't the way American backers and producers do it on Broadway. They want their party and mean to have it.

A few familiar faces were in evidence – Mel Smith (with whom I'd done a breakfast television slot some years earlier), Michael Palin, and Eddie Izzard – all of whom I liked enormously and who talked to me at length with great understanding of Morecambe and Wise.

The absence of the spirit of Morecambe and Wise – or the entire soul of the piece, as Hamish McColl puts it – from the new production was painfully emphasized by the fact that not once did the huge media contingent in atten-dance try to speak with my mother or show any remote interest in the London production which had generated the play's presence on Broadway in the first place. It would be interesting to know what film-maker Steven Spielberg made of the New York production. Allegedly he was a huge fan and devotee of the original London production and instrumental in creating the Broadway opportunity.

Kevin Kline, possibly best known to British audiences as the villain in the movie *A Fish Called Wanda*, made a good opening-night guest star and did further nights, as did other guests, such as Liam Neeson, Meryl Streep, and Glenn Close.

The play was doing OK business until America invaded Iraq. What with the recent memory of 9/11 hanging over the country like the sword of Damocles and all Broadway productions suffering as a consequence, it was only a matter of time before audiences thinned and the first-night party was just a memory. On the fateful day of the invasion of Iraq, as the play went through its machinations, a man jumped up in the audience and shouted, 'We've gone into Iraq!', to which there was the kind of 'Yee-hah!' reaction that you tend to get when Americans are together in a relatively confined space. As Hamish said to me, 'Talk about breaking the air of suspended disbelief! It took ten minutes to draw them back in.'

'As the play went through its machinations, a man jumped up in the audience and shouted, "We've gone into Iraq!"'

David Pugh hung on in there for as long as possible as the show was up for an award, but, when it didn't win, the cast and crew were soon recalled to the UK. The production was given immediate notice and, with a brief countdown to closure, they were six miles up in the sky and flying home.

It was an interesting rather than a commercially viable run – an exercise from which we perhaps all learned something, and I include myself here in my vague role as consultant to the project. And there had been time for one cheerful celebratory event before leaving New York: Kenneth Branagh married his girlfriend Lindsay. As Hamish McColl recalls, it was 'definitely one of the high moments of the run … a great memory.'

One final personal memory: I remember taking my mother to look at the splendid Grand Central Station. I'd seen it used as a location in so many films, so to actually stand there and marvel at this iconic sight was a treat beyond all other treats. A lady travelling from the station, clearly uncertain of which platform she was searching for, marched briskly up to a cop – great using that word in its appropriate context – and said, 'Oh, do excuse me, but could you tell me … ?'

'I'm sorry, madam,' interrupted the cop, gently raising his hands and giving an apologetic shrug, 'but I'm closed Sundays!' Both of them laughed loudly at this, and it reminded me of years earlier when my father had just returned from one of those Ed Sullivan shows he wrote about in his diary. 'I have to say the one thing that struck me is the native New Yorker's sense of humour,' he once told me. And now I got it first-hand.

The story of *The Play What I Wrote* didn't end in New York. In April 2007 its nationwide tour of Britain – happily back in its *original* format – concluded. And that was with its third cast since The Right Size created and starred in the show.

I still get involved with the publicity for the play whenever it's recast and up and running, occasionally visiting venues where it's due to open to talk with the press about Eric and Ernie, and about the play, its history, its metamorphosis in New York, its changing casts, and, of course, its guest stars. Sometimes I did a Q&A session with David Pugh for the touring productions. We would sit on stage in front of an invited audience and David would tell the story of how it all came together and then turn to me and ask relevant questions about Eric and Ernie to which I would give lengthy answers. We worked up quite a little double act ourselves.

In the last production I got talking with Andrew Cryer, who took on the Eric Morecambe role, while Greg Haiste played Ernie and Anthony Hoggard played Arthur and the myriad roles originally played by the great Toby Jones. Andrew recalled how, as little more than a toddler, once a week he would stay at his gran's house because his parents would go out. It must have been a weekend, because it always coincided with *The Morecambe and Wise Show* being on. He was usually allowed to watch it, but has memories of times when he wasn't supposed to: he'd sneak onto the landing and watch it through the banisters. That he should go on to portray Eric in a play seems deserved as well as ironic.

Echoing the thoughts of Hamish McColl, my own hope is that one day The Right Size will team up again to appear in the play – perhaps a special West End run, as Hamish suggests, with some mouth-watering guest stars equal to the long list of previous ones. Or, alternatively, they'll take it to somewhere else where Morecambe and Wise are recognized and hugely appreciated. I'm thinking specifically of Australia. My second wife, Jo, comes from New Zealand and has lots of family spread out across Australia, and visits we made when we were still married proved to me beyond doubt that admiration for Morecambe and Wise still exists there. I found their books and DVDs on sale in many Aussie stores.

Mentioning that part of the world, if I have one recent regret – and I certainly have too few to remember, to paraphrase Frank Sinatra – it is not taking up the opportunity to join the actors and crew of *Lord of the Rings* filming on location in New Zealand. Jo and I had planned to visit the members of her family in Australia, and a quick, seven-hour hop over to NZ would have left us watching Peter Jackson directing Orcs and Aragorn and Gandalf and Saruman and Frodo and Sam and … well, you get the idea. And to make it worse, Peter, I later learned, is a big Morecambe and Wise fan. The offer to go there had come from Andy Serkis (Gollum), whom I'd met a few times, because for some serendipitous reason we'd ended up being interviewed on the same radio programmes with indecent frequency.

The big link between *The Play What I Wrote* and the *Lord of the Rings* movies is Ian McKellen, who played Gandalf. Throughout the play The Right Size made constant remarks about him, encouraging the audience to believe that he was the permanent guest star in waiting and would soon be making his big entrance. But then Sean Foley – in Eric mode – kept explaining the actor's absence by saying, 'Can't get him out of the pub' and suchlike. When the play won an award McKellen fooled everyone by staggering on the stage behind Sean and Hamish and pretending to be drunk. Keeping up the act, he then tapped them on their shoulders mid-flow – to their huge and genuine surprise – and presented them with their award before reeling off the stage. It was another one of those nights that brought the house down.

Ken Branagh says, 'It's interesting to try and work out the mystery of what makes people laugh. I have great admiration for those comics who can stand in front of 3,000 people and make them fall about laughing – like Billy Connolly and Lee Mack. It's truly jaw-droppingly impressive.

'With Eric and Ernie and other double acts, there is the protection that comes of having a partner that guards against the loneliness out there, but there's still the basic concern of "are they going to like us tonight"? Yes, it goes with the territory but it's that which actors admire most in comedians.'

As I finished lunch with Ken Branagh, he made me smile when he told me of a play he had recently been doing – a dark, Russian tragicomedy called Ivanov. 'And for no good reason,' says Ken, 'we all start doing impressions of Eric Morecambe as we walk up and down the corridors before going on. It was a way for the cast to get themselves going; almost like a vocal exercise.'

It would seem Ken Branagh can't escape Eric Morecambe!

The Early Days
A Very Good Place to Start

'I was born in 1926 and when I was eight months old we moved to Christie Avenue into a new council house with three bedrooms and an outside loo. There was just me, my mother, Sadie, and my father, George ...'

A wonderful insight to a bygone era. Eric's wife's grandmother Mary, known as Polly.

Has there ever been an iconic entertainer who during his life generated such profound and continuous affection as Eric Morecambe? Probably not. Well, maybe Stephen Fry comes close. Mr Fry's ability to jolly along as one of us, as it were, while intellectually towering above us Gandalf-like in a world of Hobbits, is very endearing. Just as with Eric, you can't help but like Stephen. Whatever such persons' problems might be – and they're human, so they have problems – there remains this lovable, vulnerable, yet simultaneously optimistic air about them. As TV presenter Nick Owen wrote of Eric in his autobiography: 'He had the ability to make you laugh just by entering the room ...'

Eric with daughter Gail for Easter service.

Morecambe and Wise emerged from an era when a performer was slowly nurtured and judged purely on talent and not tabloid-style TV programmes bolstered by self-interested tabloid newspapers. You didn't grade Morecambe and Wise on an A–Z list – they were simply undisputed stars of the small screen, and hugely admired and loved stars at that.

The author Sidney Sheldon observed of his friend Groucho Marx, 'Even when Groucho wanted to insult someone he couldn't, because no one would take the insult seriously.' That straightaway makes me think of my father and his forays into attempting to be serious – which he would have enjoyed more frequently had people been able to take him more seriously. But as well as being plain and simple Dad, he was plainly and simply hilarious almost all the time. Part of it was his nature and part was the burden he carried of not wishing to disappoint anyone. Being a living comic legend was certainly a two-edged sword.

Although I'm now in my fifties it all seems so incredibly recent and fresh in my mind. But that's the Morecambe and Wise effect; that's what living with such a master of comedy does to you – it preserved the moments as they occurred. And I know I'm not alone. People still come up to me in the street and say, 'It must be nearly ten years since your dad died.' And when I say, 'No. It's nearer a quarter of a century,' a look of incredulity sweeps across their face.

'Being a living comic legend was certainly a two-edged sword.'

The one thing that I knew so little about until very, very recently was my father's own humble beginnings. Then, while recording a spot for a TV company filming in Lancashire, I was introduced to a few people who remembered him. One such person is Roger Obertelli, who, as a kid, along with his elder brother Kenneth, would play football with Eric in their street, Christie Avenue, More-

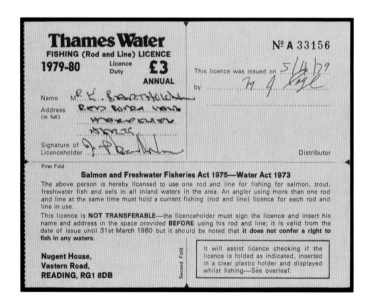
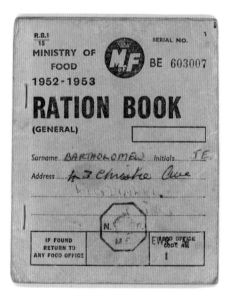

A fishing licence and ration book, both showing rare occasions on which Eric signed with his real birth name of John Eric Bartholomew.

cambe. Roger and his wife, now in their later years, remarkably have settled back in that same street.

He explained to me how all the kids in the street would be playing football in the late afternoon when suddenly Eric's mother, Sadie, would appear and whisk him indoors. Ten minutes later a rather solemn Eric would re-emerge dressed in top hat and tails. With a plaintiff wave of the hand, he would saunter off down the street and across what were then open fields stretching into the distance on his way to the dance and music lessons that Sadie broke her back to fund. Roger says that they would all chuckle at Eric's departing figure and can recall his frustration at having to leave their game of football. But you sense from Roger that now there is an air of 'Well, he had the last laugh, didn't he?'

Eric once outlined his own upbringing. His account could have been composed by or for the Lancashire tourist board, but it's a genuine personal look at the seaside town's life through the seasons by Eric as he recalled the early part of the previous century:

> I was born in 1926 and when I was eight months old we moved to Christie Avenue into a new council house with three bedrooms and an outside loo. There was just me, my mother, Sadie, and my father, George . . . We were working class, but comfortable, even though Dad earned only £2 a week in my youth. He worked for the council . . . Mother supplemented our income, particularly when I began dancing lessons. She used to scrub floors and work as an usherette at the pier theatre. I had four special friends, all of us football fanatics; we supported Preston North End and Morecambe FC. We went to all Morecambe's games for the simple reason that we got in to see them for nothing by the somewhat devious method of bending the railings that surrounded the ground . . . One of our favourite haunts was a sweet shop loftily named Halfway House. It was run by one of the biggest men I have ever seen. I can't remember his name, but he was at least six feet six inches tall . . .
>
> Apart from the normal run of goodies at Halfway House, there was a kind of board covered in paper and on it were dozens of black spots. You paid

Mr 'Bigman' a halfpenny and he gave you a pencil which you forced into a black spot. If there was a number underneath, you won a prize. But there weren't many numbers.

At home my favourite foods were shrimps, black puddings and tripe – the latter delicacies having been a staple diet for comedians' material for years! I also loved mushrooms, which my father and I would pick from the fields around our home. But one delicacy – the taste remains with me still – was 'cocoa dip'. Every morning my mother would mix a quantity of cocoa powder and sugar in a bag. The idea was to have the bag open in my coat pocket and keep dipping a wet finger into the mixture … It was like nectar!

When the summer came Morecambe became a different place. It was like being brought up to date; finding out what was going on in the world. You never saw many cars in those days, yet August brought a veritable motorcade of Austin Sevens and Morris Eights driven by the 'well-to-do', paying their three pounds a week, full board at the town's desirable residences …

On the sands entertainment was provided by the Nigger Minstrels, then undeterred by the racial overtones of their title.

As the darkness came at summer's end, there were the illuminations. Happy Mount Park was a fairyland and as the holidaymakers took their final glimpse of annual escape, I would warm with the thought of good things to come: Autumn and Bonfire night, winter with slides on the footpath and scarcely any rain. Spring with the town reawakening, the annual Carnival that had a West End polish to it and the grand influx of the immigrants from the mill towns, the Scots and the Midlanders. Summer again with its boat trips, bathing beauty contests and the ever-present Nigger Minstrels …

Obviously I knew my father intimately, and I sense the above was purposely drawn up in a Charles-Dickens-meets-Perry-Como way as he rendered his thoughts into print. My father could be very lacklustre when talking about his childhood days in Morecambe, but *writing* about them seems to have focused his mind. Certainly Eric returned often enough to the north, particularly to spend time with his parents, which my sister and I enjoyed enormously too. But it never really felt like Morecambe was his home – that this was the place that had not just given rise to its greatest son, but had lent its name to him as a vehicle for his success. I also sensed that the longer he spent away from the county of his birth – which, excepting the occasional holidays, was most of the time as our family was based in the south – the more uncertain he felt about it whenever he returned. It was a little like he wasn't sure how to behave, because there were so many friends and family who knew Eric Morecambe before comedy did.

'Certainly Eric returned often enough to the north … but it never really felt like Morecambe was his home.'

A couple of years ago, while in Morecambe filming for the BBC series *Comedy Map of Great Britain,* I had the honour and pleasure of being taken on the official 'Eric Morecambe Tour'. We visited all the significant sights from Eric's youth. It was wonderful, though the strange thought hit me that the last time I did the tour was with Eric himself, decades before it even existed as a tourist walk. Back in 1968 or 1969, while staying with my grandparents, my father said he'd take me on a stroll down memory lane. He was very helpful, pointing out this and that significant building from his childhood. We even passed what had once been the cinema where he'd chucked fruit and veg down from the balcony onto bald-headed targets, and the address where he'd trundled off to for those music and dance lessons. Then there were the schools, the shops, and even the optician's where he'd been eye-tested for his first pair of glasses. What struck me at the time, but much more now decades later as I write

4. NORTHUMBERLAND S.T
MORECAMBE

On the right are Eric's mother and father, while on the left are Eric's uncle Jack and auntie Alice. The address of the photographer is printed at the foot of card, showing that it was just walking distance from where they lived.

this book, is how dispassionate he was about it all. He didn't dawdle lost in reminiscence. There was nothing rose-tinted about his memories: it was all quite brisk, almost as if he was explaining what had happened to someone else he had known incredibly well, but definitely not his own personal history.

Then suddenly it occurred to me that he *was* someone else back then, so the third-person approach to his childhood was quite comprehensible. John Eric Bartholomew had shed his identity to reveal the comic genius Eric Morecambe. And at the same time, and on that same walk, I came to notice how diluted his northern accent had become. He had more what writer-comedian Ben Elton calls his transatlantic accent, something both he and Ernie were especially fond of displaying in their musical numbers. His accent had become quite hard to place: certainly pure Lancastrian didn't immediately spring to mind.

When I was a boy and Eric's career was just starting to blossom, his northern tones – his birth signature – were very strong. 'Grass', 'bath', and 'laugh' had the same vowel sound as 'ass', and 'look', 'book', and 'cook' rhymed with the American way of saying 'duke'. His parents would retain these pronunciations for the rest of their days (understandably, considering it was where they lived their whole lives), but I sensed with my father that he was a man of the planet, not a specific country, county, or town. In a way it gave him a sense of mystery, for while northern traits clung on in his accent, they were more evident in his delivery of a funny line than in everyday conversation. If anything,

Ernie retained his Yorkshire accent much more than Eric did his Lancastrian one, though both had taken on that same transatlantic twang.

'He once told me that he was very torn as a kid between loyalty to his mates ... and loyalty to his mother's dream.'

This was something I hadn't given much thought to until writing about film legend Cary Grant. He had started life as Archibald Leach of Bristol, England. Yet if anyone ever changed his name and identity so completely it was Grant. And I soon discovered that to many Americans he was believed to be one of theirs. Except for the big Cary Grant followers, the majority assumed he was born and bred in America. And Eric adored Grant's poise, style, chic. He was a personal friend of Grant's and I can imagine how affected he would have been by this luminary of the film industry. Maybe some of it rubbed off on Eric, who

Eric on stage performing his solo act for Jack Hylton's Youth Takes A Bow tour during which he first met and later teamed up with a young Ernie Wise.

was often described as classy. Ernie once told me that when Eric looked in the mirror he saw Cary Grant. There is a logical link here.

Despite the happy memories – real or invented – depicted in the piece he penned on Morecambe, I know this to have been a difficult time for the young Eric. He once told me that he was very torn as a kid between loyalty to his mates, all of them having childhood aspirations to become footballing legends like Tom Finney and Stanley Matthews, and loyalty to his mother's dream of his getting a working act together and so improving his lot in life by following the showbiz path. He must have had shrewdness about him from an early age, for while he continued to push on his football – leading to the offer of a trial with a League club – he recognized the potentially greater longevity of a career in theatrical entertainment compared with one in football. One injury and that was it, and back then it was not a well-paid profession for even the top players, and he knew he was not good enough to be a top player.

But this is jumping the gun. The young Eric still had plenty of boyish mischief to burn off before the days of theatre and football really took a grip. And most of that energy was expended with his cousin George Trelfall, always known as 'Sonny'.

The Bash Street Kids

'No-one ever believes this, but my mother would have always verified it for me. My earliest recollection is of when I was nine months old.'

Michael Palin, in his published diaries *The Python Years*, describes my father perfectly. Palin is at a party at the BBC in 1972 which is full of showbiz celebrities, Eric among them. 'Eric Morecambe is another one who never dropped his comic persona all evening,' he writes. 'If one talked to him, or if one heard him talking to anyone else, he was always doing a routine. He has a very disconcerting habit of suddenly shouting at the top of his voice at some-one only a foot away.' While Palin puts in print what is genuinely recognized but rarely remarked upon, I would just add that my father not dropping his comic persona and speaking loudly at close quarters was not reserved just for evenings out. It's difficult to think of a time when he wasn't 'on'. Add that to the lifestyle of his chosen career, and really it's no wonder he ended up seri-ously ill and leaving us so prematurely. Later in his book Palin mentions that he'd heard Eric loved his BBC TV series *Ripping Yarns* but would never be able to verify if that was true. Well, if you happen to read this Michael, it *is* true. Eric adored the series and often I would sit down with him at the family home and we'd watch it.

Eric as this rather disconcerting, loud, and boisterous adult was not, it seems, so very different as a child. A little more refined in later years, perhaps, as we already know how as a boy he would misbehave at the local cinema.

A wonderful photo of (left to right) Eric's father George, 'Sonny' Threlfall, who was Eric's cousin, and Eric. The baby is Michael Threlfall, 'Wiggy', and is 'Sonny's' child. Wiggy, who is now in his sixties and still resides in Morecambe, has remained a firm friend, and we spent time together at the Morecambe v Luton match in March 2009. A lifelong fan of the Shrimps, he has many tales to tell of Eric, some which appear in this book.

Interviewing him in 1982 I asked my father to recall some of his childhood memories. This wasn't something he normally discussed at length, but I caught him on a good day when he was feeling somewhat sprightly in his tweed jacket and bow-tie, with an endless Havana cigar protruding from his mouth in a meerschaum holder – a kind of Lord Grade pose. The sun was shining through his office window on his portable typewriter, where all his work was key-hammered onto A4 for posterity, and that day he was well up to a bit of gentle reflection:

> *No-one ever believes this, but my mother would have always verified it for me.*
> *My earliest recollection is of when I was nine months old. I remember being put*
> *on the kitchen table in our home in Buxton Street, to be wrapped in a coat and*

long scarf before being taken out in my pushchair. I can also remember that the roof of that house had caved in, and that was why we were the first on the list to be moved to Christie Avenue by the council.

I only know as far back as my great-grandfather on my Dad's side, who brought his family to Lancashire from what was then Westmorland, but is now Cumbria. So we have been Lancastrians for approximately a hundred and fifty years or so. By coincidence, my grandparents on my mother's side were also from Westmorland, but came down some years afterwards.

I remember making an inkwell at school during woodwork lessons – we didn't call them carpentry lessons in those days, you know. I could have been no older than seven or eight. This inkwell that I proudly presented to my parents was in fact just a plain lump of wood with a hole skewered in the middle. You couldn't have put any ink in it. It was terrible! But my mother thought it was brilliant. 'Oh lovely, Eric,' she said when I gave it to her. Then she called my Dad. 'Look, George. Come and see what our Eric has made.' She actually kept it, along with many similar items, throughout her lifetime.

I remember once going with the family on a picnic to Hest Bank [on the edge of Morecambe]. I was ten at the time but I really remember it as though it was this morning. I would have to wear a blazer suit if I was going to look my best. That was short blue flannel trousers and a blue flannel jacket. We were standing at the bus stop waiting to go home when a thunderstorm started and it poured with rain. The whole of my suit seemed to become sponge-like, soaking up the rain as it fell. I began wiping the rain from my face and hands and legs with my jacket sleeves, but it wasn't just rain – it was blue dye pouring out of my suit. By the time I got home I was blue from head to foot.

I often have a chuckle to myself when I recollect some of my father's endeavours. There was a time when I was a boy when I would sit and watch him catch starlings. He used a dustbin lid and a stick with a piece of string connected to it. Then he would put a lump of bread under the lid and use the stick to support it. When the starling went to have a nibble, he would pull the string and trap the poor little thing. He would catch between ten and twenty of these birds, kill them, then give them to my Auntie Maggie to bake in a pie. She needed about twenty, because when you pluck a starling you're not looking at too much flesh. I once had an airgun as a lad and he borrowed it to shoot a seagull off our neighbour's roof. He hit it cleanly enough, but it toppled straight down their chimney pot and into the fireplace round which the family were gathered at the time. That must have given them some shock.

I can recall walking with my mother by the river that weaves its way through Hest Bank. I was fifteen, and she turned to me and said, 'Now one day you'll be a big star, as long you don't get big-headed. But when you are a big star, you will buy me a house in Hest Bank, won't you?'

I nodded dumbly, and said, 'Yes, Mam; I'll buy you a house out here.'

Many years later, in the latter part of the sixties, whenever I saw her she would say, 'Well you are a big star, and now where's my house you promised me at Hest Bank?' And eventually I bought her a home in Hest Bank.

School photo. Eric is in the front row, second from left.

Before and during these times remembered from his childhood days, my father was being his lively self, usually in the company of his biggest mate and cousin, George 'Sonny' Trelfall.

'Seeing Eric go off to dance class meant we all gave him a hard time ... but it was the right thing for him without a doubt.'

Like Eric, Sonny was a bundle of fun, mischief, humour, and constant laughter. Recently I was speaking with Sonny's son, Michael (known to all as Wiggy – nicknames were seemingly obligatory in the Trelfall family), who is now sixty. Born, bred, and still living in Morecambe, he's someone I've known all my life but never discussed the early days with very much. But talking to him now I learned that when Eric first decided to embark on a career in entertainment he approached Sonny to see if he wanted to form a double act with him. 'But my dad,' said Wiggy, totally unfazed by the notion of what might have been, 'couldn't really be bothered, you know. I mean, he thought it sounded like very hard work – all a bit tiring. And it wasn't his thing. It wasn't really *anyone*'s thing back then if you were a bloke. My dad went into the Army instead at that time.' This was echoed by Alan Hodgson, who went to the same school as Eric but knew him more through being a neighbour and great friend of his cousin Sonny. 'There's nothing more cruel than kids,' he explained, 'and seeing Eric go off to dance class meant we all gave him a hard time. I don't know how he did it. But it was the right thing for him without a doubt, considering the rest of his career.' This was said with genuine honesty, something I would find in great supply on my research trip to Morecambe. Those still living who knew my father have such respect for what he achieved. There was never an ounce of envy or affectation shown to me.

Wiggy gave me a picture of my father that implied there were two Erics – the kid doing dance class and the kid who kicked a ball around and was one of the lads from the Christie Avenue estate. 'Uncle Eric and my dad were never bad as such, but they were always up to mischief,' he said. 'They'd take Auntie Sadie's jam pots, empty them out, go back to the shop and claim the refund on the jars.

'But my dad was thrilled for Uncle Eric,' Wiggy went on in his strong Lancashire accent. 'He always thought he had it in him. And when Uncle Eric visited they would get together and laugh and laugh. All his life my dad would make your dad laugh.'

And he's right! I remember my father telling me as much. That shared camaraderie of childhood never goes away. Former school and dance class friend Betty Ford remembers it well. 'I think Eric enjoyed talking about the old times and seeing familiar faces,' she said. Betty recalls my father with genuine fondness. 'He would just shuffle into school, his hands deep in his pockets, totally unconcerned that he might be late for lessons. He was moonlighting, of course – doing his showbiz stuff most evenings, so was always a bit tired. He was definitely quite slovenly in appearance. But he was a very popular lad at school. I wouldn't say he was a cheerful personality, because he looked so tired in the mornings.'

The co-ed system worked slightly differently back in the thirties, Betty

HARPENDEN.

DEAR MICHEAL,
MAY WE SAY, MANY HAPPY RETURNS". I REMEMBER TWENTY YEARS AGO, CARRYING YOU AROUND MOSS LANE, WEN I COULDN'T EVEN LIFT YOU. ENCLOSED IS A CHEQUE FROM US, I SUGGEST YOU BUY A NEW PLAYER FOR MORECAMBE, AND PUT £19 IN THE BANK.

LOVE FROM ERIC, JOHN, GAIL, x GARY.

P.S.
YOU NEEDN'T CALL ME UNCLE ANYMORE - IT MAKES ME FEEL OLD.

A letter from Eric to Michael Threlfall (a.k.a. 'Wiggy'). Eric kept in touch with Sonny, his cousin and Michael's father, throughout his life.

explained. 'It's interesting to recall that back then the girls and boys were split up at school. We were literally segregated and I would talk to Eric through the railings. It was like a mixed school, but you weren't really allowed to mix much, although you could in classes except for the last year, where it was boys- and girls-only classes. I think they didn't want us to socialize with each other.' With a smile she said, 'It's not like that now, of course. And they've brought the railings down.'

And what of those very average school reports that brought his mother, Sadie, close to apoplexy? 'Well, Eric certainly wasn't academic,' recalled Betty, with wonderful understatement. 'He could be very lazy. But he got on all right, though. And he was mischievous, yet in a quiet sort of way, if you know what I mean.' I certainly do know what she means: that quiet mischievousness never left him; indeed it is the best way one can describe his antics around the family and the home and his working persona as half of Morecambe and Wise. 'But he wasn't a loudmouth sort of lad,' Betty added. 'He kept to himself quite a bit.'

And what about the teachers who must have felt very let down by my father's lack of contribution to school life? 'The teachers, in fact, thought a great deal about him,' Betty told me. 'I saw some of them a while after leaving school and they were all very fond of him.'

I was interested to get a sense of what Eric's success meant to these childhood friends. 'We were all thrilled for him,' said Betty, cautiously adding, 'Of course, his mother did push him hard, though.' It wouldn't be the last time I would hear this during my visit to Lancashire.

I was keen to learn a little more about Eric's dancing lessons, which would go on to serve his career so well. On this subject Betty was a good starting point, considering she went to the Royal Ballet School and in later years started a chain of her own dance schools.

'It was mostly through dancing that I got to know Eric,' she said. 'Eric went to Mrs Hunter's dancing school, and I went to the Plaza School of Dancing. But we did dance together. We danced at the Mickey Mouse Club sometimes.'

The Mickey Mouse Club, Betty explained, was a Saturday morning cinema club at the local Odeon, where kids paid sixpence to watch a movie – like a *Flash Gordon* feature starring Buster Crabbe – and then danced on the stage to music.

'Me and Eric would sometimes leave together afterwards and go back to his house on Christie Avenue, because it backed on to the football ground. In those days, before all the stands were built, we could watch the Saturday home matches through his bedroom window.'

Then Betty gave me an insight into Eric's home town in the late thirties. 'It was wartime, and Morecambe was full of RAF. So we used to go round doing shows at all these churches where they had clubs for the RAF personnel billeted in and around the town. Eric used to entertain them, too, but I remember him as a dancer and not a comedian, though it was more as a comedian that he did his entertaining even back then. This would have been about the time he met Ernie Wise.'

Betty remembered inviting Eric to her birthday party at her house. 'He tried to teach me how to wink, and I still can't do it. We used to play this game where the girls are sitting on chairs with the boys behind, and whoever they want to kiss they wink at, and then they change places. It was my twelfth birthday, and I think why I remember it so well is that Eric brought me some perfume and a handkerchief.'

It became clear to me that all these old school friends of my father's that I was slowly getting to meet and interview for this book had remained in contact with one another. And that, as Betty pointed out, was mostly because they had stayed in the area. 'But I didn't see your father for years after he left,' she said. 'Then one day a relation of your father's told me that he was coming to More-cambe and that he really wanted to see me. He turned up in his Rolls-Royce at my husband's chemist shop. He stayed a couple of hours. He told me he hadn't someone whom he could just call on to see for a cup of coffee.'

Eric also made other visits to the area, Wiggy told me. 'He would sometimes come and watch Morecambe play at Christie Park. He'd be wearing a long coat and a deerstalker. You couldn't recognize him, which is just what he wanted. But I'd go up to him anyway and say, "Hi, Uncle Eric," and he'd put a finger to his lips. "Shh!" he'd go. "I want to watch the match without being noticed. Don't give me away."'

Wiggy added that my father would try to visit old familiar faces in the neighbourhood. 'Mr Lee was one of them. Eric, now a big star, would stand awkwardly in his sitting room while Mr Lee would be in his armchair puffing on a pipe. After a while, Mr Lee said, "Eee – I don't know what it is they find funny in thee, lad!"'

My father also returned to Morecambe when Wiggy was working on a building site. 'One of the lads exclaimed, "Look! It's Eric Morecambe down there. Would you believe it?" I smiled to myself and said, "Oh yes, so it is. Well, I think I'll go down and have a crack with him and see how he is." They looked at me flabbergasted – they had no idea of the connection. So I went down and said quietly, "Hi, Uncle Eric." Your dad gave me a smile and then a big hug. The lads on the site couldn't believe what they were seeing from above. Hilarious.'

'I remember him as a dancer and not a comedian, though it was more as a comedian that he did his entertaining even back then.'

I was reminded of a visit Eric made to Hest Bank in the early seventies. By now his parents were living in the village. He dropped in on a neighbour and purely by coincidence *The Morecambe and Wise Show* was on TV. 'Oh great!' said my father. 'Do you mind if I watch it for a bit?' The neighbour said that was fine and went to make them a cup of tea. At that point the neighbour's son turned up with his mates and wandered into the sitting room to be confronted by the sight of Eric Morecambe sitting there in his house with a cup of tea in hand watching his own TV show. A surreal moment.

Wiggy made the interesting point that Eric used aspects of his northern upbringing in routines on *The Morecambe and Wise Show*. 'I don't know if everyone noticed it,' he said, 'but every now and then you would see a character and think,

UPON THE OCCASION OF THE UNVEILING OF THE PLAQUE AT NO. 43 CHRISTIE AVENUE

There's a bloke we all love, name of Eric,
One half of Morecambe and Wise,
They left us a wonderful legacy,
Of laughter and tears in our eyes,

Eric took his name from the town where he lived,
For "Morecambe" seemed just the thing,
Thank God he didn't come from Littlehampton,
It doesn't have quite the same ring,

It was in Christie Ave that Eric grew up,
The childhood before the big journey,
That's why we commemorate the house with a plaque,
From the loyal fans of Eric and Ernie,

So thank you a million, Eric, our pal,
For the sunshine you brought through the years,
And though you're not with us, we all watch you still,
And once more share the laughter and tears.

**Presented to the fans of Eric and Ernie
by Bernard Wrigley, 14th July 1999**

Christie Avenue, the Morecambe street where Eric grew up playing football with his mates as a child. It was here that his mother would call him in to the house to adorn his top hat and tails for his dancing classes. On the right of the picture can be seen a yellow plaque commemorating the fact that Eric lived here in his youth.

"I know exactly who that's supposed to be." One character was the pigeon-keeper Eric pretended to be in a Thames TV show he and Ernie did. That was based on someone in Morecambe. So, too, the character he portrays walking across the back of the stage at the end of the show wearing a long coat, cloth cap, and carrying a big bag. These people existed,' Wiggy assured me. 'I *knew* these people.'

It seems Morecambe was a small world in many ways back then. After Eric and his parents left 43 Christie Avenue, where Eric had spent so many years of his childhood, to move to a new but still local address, Wiggy's parents, Sonny and Ethel, moved in. If that isn't keeping it in the family!

'It seems the young Eric tried quite hard to keep up with his older mates.'

It was at Christie Avenue that Eric nearly died in an 'accident'. 'They were playing Cowboys and Indians,' explained Wiggy. 'Eric, being the youngest of the gang, got to be the fall guy, and was the one chosen to be lynched. My dad and others stood him on a dustbin with a rope around his neck. When they pushed him off and left him dangling, Auntie Sadie happened to glance out the window and rushed outside. She gave them a hard time for that. She went absolutely berserk, my dad told me years later. To be honest, Auntie Sadie used to scare me a bit. I think we were all a bit frightened of her.'

It seems the young Eric tried quite hard to keep up with his older mates. 'All the young kids wore short trousers,' Wiggy recalled. 'But Eric got Sadie to cut a piece of cloth and make him some long ones so he could walk tall with the others.'

For me it was hard to appreciate what Morecambe had been like in those days. Wiggy described it as 'a lively little place back then', adding that, 'It was the holiday package industry that started to kill it. But it's coming back again now.' And he's right. There's been a huge financial injection, particularly along the sea front. The Midland Hotel, the Art Deco pride of Morecambe, has been

completely renovated by the developer Urban Splash and opened in the summer of 2008. The Eric Morecambe Statue and the memorial area it occupies has apparently increased tourism to the area by nearly thirty per cent. There have been great efforts to invigorate the region's wildlife and bird-watching attractions, the pier has gone, replaced by a modern stone jetty, and sand has been delivered by the ton to at last give Morecambe the kind of beach visitors to Blackpool have taken for granted for over a century of sea-bathing.

What captured my imagination was that in Morecambe there had been a community of children who played and learned together, swearing and daring one another on, struggling for rank and status, inventing elaborate games for which none of today's technology was necessary; exploring their surroundings and waging mock battles with their rival peers. It was a time of dirty knees, torn pullovers, collarless shirts, leather shoes with soles worn paper-thin from years spent running down streets kicking cans and stones and one another. This was the hand-me-down era, when words like 'fashion' and 'trends' were the last words you would hear on most people's lips. This was the New York Bronx world of outer Lancaster.

top left **The author's sons and nephew (left to right: Henry, Arthur, Jack and Adam) cavort with their grandfather.**

top right **The Queen unveils Eric in Morecambe Bay, summer 1999.**

I caught a glimpse of that era when I returned to Christie Avenue to take a little look at the front of the house where Eric had lived, and the street where Eric had played football and set off to dance classes.

'The Eric Morecambe Statue and the memorial area it occupies has apparently increased tourism to the area by nearly thirty per cent.'

My father recorded in his own words how as a kid he would go fishing with his dad in Morecambe Bay. They would get up at daybreak and Eric would perch on the back of George's bicycle as he pedalled them down to the sea front (just in front of where Eric's statue now stands). And, as Wiggy told me, 'Eric's dad, George, made his own fish hooks. He would often fish in the big basin of deep water right next to the old bridge at Hest Bank. He was always going on about this huge pike he knew that lurked down there. "I had it on my line once, but it got away," he would say. I don't think he ever caught it.'

was taken. Patricia Gerrard, née Goodyear, remembers how her late husband, Frank, would take Eric fishing both as boy and man. Frank, who would eventually become chief director of a Morecambe trawling company, and Eric were old school friends. The trawlers are responsible for bringing in the famous Morecambe shrimps, along with various kinds of fish. 'Eric was addicted to potted shrimps,' recalled Patricia. 'In the early years, when Eric was at the Winter Gardens, he wasn't quite as famous nationally as he later became, but in Morecambe he was very well known. And Morecambe in those days was heaving with people, it was that busy, and they used to crowd to see Eric.'

Patricia recalls Eric visiting her and her husband at the trawlermen's market. 'They had to close the doors when he visited there, that many people were trying to get to him.' I pictured my father's reaction to the situation being, 'They

Taken in the mid to late sixties, it is hard to pin-point where exactly this photo was taken. Eric has clearly landed a fair-sized fish, and it is just possible that this was one of his many outings on the River Test. The other man is unknown.

were an angry mob who'd just seen my act!' Patricia continued, 'I walked up to him and he grabbed my arm and said to the others, "You haven't met my wife, Patricia. The best catch of the season!" Later I started musing about what the future might hold. Eric looked at me and said in the voice of a weatherman, "Wet at night, warm and close, then later a little son!"

'What my husband and Eric did back then was to hire a boat so they could do a day's fishing and get away from the crowds. Apparently Eric was hilarious all the time. My husband tried to get the boat out and it drifted sideways and Eric teased, "Are you sure you know how to work this thing!"'

Patricia also told me about Eric and Frank as kids. 'They were both into wildlife, including frogs, newts and insects: anything to do with the outdoors. There was an Auntie Harriet on my husband's side who the boys visited occasionally. She always wore a big hat with a large brim around it. Eric would say, "I like the brooch on your hat, Aunt Harriet." And the 'brooch' would start running around the brim. It would be a small frog, or something. She'd shriek and catch it and Eric and Frank would run outside and down the street in hysterics.'

Like Eric's old school friend Betty Ford, Patricia would go to the Mickey Mouse Club. The dancing that would follow the Saturday morning film show I find a strange concept to get my head around when nowadays we have access to so many forms of entertainment. Patricia remembered Betty being a superb dancer, and Betty herself told me that when Eric returned to Morecambe in the early seventies and bumped into her, he was surprised to find she hadn't left the area. 'He thought I'd have gone on to have an amazing dancing career around the world,' she says, 'but it was teaching that interested me.'

'When he was a boy, Eric used to go to the dance school in Queen Street with Betty,' Patricia said. 'The Co-op was down there, and the late, great actress Thora Hird, then a young girl, but a couple of years older than Eric, would be in the window in a kiosk "selling fags", as she put it. Eric would come down the street on the way to the dance school, and Thora would shout out to him and ask him how the dance lessons were going. They never really had the chance to become friends, possibly because of the age difference, but they were both more than aware of the other and destined for the same profession.'

'Eric was the star of the production – always. His tap dancing was brilliant.'

Patricia remembered the dance school itself as being one floor in a building of floor upon floor. 'In this dance school, Eric came on brilliantly because of Betty's ability. That was a huge influence on him. Then Betty told me one day, "Guess what? Eric's going to London, and he wants me to go with him!" I smiled and said, "You'd better be careful, then." I mean, not many people went off to London like that back then. And Betty didn't go with him, and Eric set off on what would become his career.

'Betty and I reflected on those times years later. "Wasn't that Eric Morecambe a laugh as a boy," we'd say. And he was, because he would be so funny even when he was dancing with Betty at the Mickey Mouse Club.'

Eventually, as part of a redevelopment plan, the Co-op and the Royalty Theatre came down, and they built an Arndale Centre in its place. Eric was asked to open it, which he did. 'You should have seen the crowds,' said Patricia. 'Eric had to cut the ribbon with a giant pair of scissors, which was a funny sight straight off. Then he said, "This looks like a big house!" Then he pointed to the shining new escalators and said, "They've even got an escalator going to your bedroom!"'

Nora Longfield is another former school and dance class friend of my father's who still lives in Morecambe. 'I wasn't in his class as he was younger than me,' she told me. 'I remember him there, of course, because we used to get on the bus for the same school but at different stops. Sometimes he would come and sit with me, and sometimes he wouldn't, depending on how he felt.'

It was through the dance classes that Nora got to know my father, and looking back she described him as a comedian from the outset. 'Wherever he was, whatever he was doing, he made you laugh. There was a gang of us who used to go to the Floral Hall together to the Saturday night dance. We'd dance together – ballroom-dance – and Eric couldn't do it at all: he had two left feet.' This I found interesting as his own father was an accomplished ballroom dancer. 'The rest of his dancing, and what he was learning at dance classes, was unbelievable,' Nora went on. 'At school we couldn't wait for him to do his bit for the Christmas Show, which was part of the festive celebrations. He would do his dance in top hat and tails with a cane. We all adored it and looked forward to it. Eric was the star of the production – always. His tap dancing was brilliant. Just because the ballroom dancing wasn't his thing didn't stop us dancing with him because we knew invariably he'd make us laugh. He'd always come out with something very, very funny and have us in fits. It was in his nature.

'Later, when we all left school, we drifted apart and we never crossed paths again, although I always sensed he was someone who never forgot his roots. He came back more than people realized, because often we'd hear about it through someone, like my daughter, telling us they'd spotted him out and about.'

As I sat in Nora's small but comfortable home at Hest Bank, a house and a world not unlike those of all my father's contemporaries that I was privileged to meet on my visit, I couldn't help but ask her if Eric's remarkable rise to stardom had surprised her.

'No, not at all,' she answered at once. 'It was almost obvious what was going to happen, as the talent was there from such a young age. It would have almost been stranger had it *not* happened. He took it in his stride. And his mother was a big part of his success; she pushed him, but he must have loved to do it really, or he wouldn't have done it. For instance, those school performances: it should be remembered he volunteered for them.

'But despite the passing years, you never forget someone like Eric. It's just that you end up on different tracks in life. That's just the way it is.'

Meet the Folks

'My great mistake, until I was shown the error of my ways, was in always being in too much of a hurry. My mother's name for me was perfect – Jifflearse. All I wanted was to take in as much as I could in as short a time as possible ...'

The author flanked by loving parents.

Eric's father was one of the loveliest men you could wish to meet; one of those easy-going, uncomplicated sorts. George worked for the Corporation and his was a very different upbringing from that of his only child. By choosing, or being taken down, depending on how you view these things, his road to fame and fortune, Eric had to rock boats in the process of that journey. George never did, and I think Eric vaguely resented the fact that his father had been able to avoid any such confrontations in his life.

George came from a large family of some six brothers and two sisters, so he had probably learned much about sibling rivalry and pecking order and emerged from that experience per-haps a shade more grounded and tolerant than his own son would turn out. For the inner peacefulness that George so clearly possessed never really rubbed off on Eric, who lacked tolerance and admitted as much himself. As Sadie and George's only child, and as a talented lad on top of it all, Eric simply became accustomed to getting things his own way. This didn't mean he grew up either difficult or selfish – he was simply intolerant of anything that might have jarred with him. And it accounts for his inability to see the grey areas of life – for him everything was either black or white, which was quite frustrating to live around. Not just for me as his son: I mean difficult for everyone close to him, including his parents and his friends, who had the earliest experience of this side of him.

Sadie was not as laid-back as George, but more tolerant than Eric. I recall her being the one in the middle who, while she had a gift for encouraging her son's talent, was also able to sit back and quite comfortably share George's less pressured pace of life. Sadie had no dreams of personal gain – ever. And, in her pivotal position in this family of three, she never lost her ability to both soothe and reprimand Eric, which she did until the day she died. Indeed the day she died she was still in control of both Eric and herself. She managed to wait for her son to return from work. He sat down and said a few brief words to her, then she sighed and that was it – gone!

Through visiting surviving relatives I have come to sense that her support and advice stretched far beyond the reach of her husband and son – that she actively advised others who went to her with a problem, particularly if it was a financial problem as she was good with both money and figures.

Her closeness to George was complemented by their differences in some unarranged, unspoken yet mutually understood way, so that harmony would always reign despite whatever the external influences of any given day. They loved each other enormously. Sadie was devoted to George, though she could sound tough on him at times, and George subservient to her every need and whim, and quite content that it should be that way. What they and their son shared as a family was a wonderful sense of humour.

George, who met Sadie at a dance at Morecambe's Winter Gardens Theatre, never stopped dancing until late in life. He would religiously attend ballroom

left A very early photo of Eric. Eric is on the far left of the front row next to his mother, Sadie. To the right is his cousin, Sonny. On the back row, looming large, is Eric's father George.

right A very young Bing Crosby being chauffeured by one of Eric's uncles who had emigrated to the States in the 1920s.

dances with a dance partner, which never concerned Sadie, who wasn't particular interested in ballroom dancing. But George, I recently learned, would also sometimes get involved in local talent competitions, just like his son.

'There was a building, the Old Tower Ballroom near the Town Hall,' Patricia Gerrard told me. 'Your grandfather, George, was a very good whistler.' I hardly needed reminding of the fact – he hardly ever *stopped* whistling. 'Eric thought he and his dad should enter a whistling competition that was on at the Ballroom. Eric and George had a great relationship, and they would tease each other. Anyway, in the end George decided to go it alone because he was the whistler of the family. He won first prize. George was thrilled, and Sadie was even more thrilled and had a party. Eric was a little perplexed, really. It was *his* job to win talent contests, and just beforehand he'd told his dad, "Oh, you haven't got a chance of winning."'

My own memories of Sadie are all positive, but my father always told me that Sadie was far softer on her grandchildren – my sister and I – than ever she was on him. And I can believe that because it is tougher to be the parent in the driving seat than the grandparent in the passenger seat. Even when Eric was in his forties, I can recall Sadie always having the last word with him – and he'd listen. I never once saw him get truly angry or even argumentative with her, because all she needed to do was raise the level of her voice a touch and he'd

A lone figure in the Austrian Alps. Eric, who was never interested in snow sports, found himself holidaying in Kitzbuhel with his wife Joan in February 1975. He didn't ski, but enjoyed taking a ski-cat (motorized sled) for a fast burn down the hills.

melt into silence. Yet this suggests some kind of matriarchal nightmare figure, which Sadie plainly was not. She was an amusing, bright, quick-witted woman – a great raconteur with many bizarre songs and stories to entertain her doting grandchildren. But, as Eric put it, 'She was no mug!' He also told me that without his mother's total confidence in his talent and her determination to see him achieve as much as he could with it, he would not have amounted to anything. 'I'd be working behind the counter at the local grocer's now,' he told me. 'Not that I'm knocking it,' he added thoughtfully, 'but it ain't the same as being a top comedian.'

In my own mother's view, 'Sadie was a very determined lady. She always knew what she wanted. She knew what she thought was right and what she thought was wrong, and you weren't going to make her waver. Although tremendously content with her life, in a way she was in the wrong environ-

left **Left to right: the author with his sister, Gail. In 2002 we tried to re-create this photo but with mixed results!**

right **Eric with adopted son Steven, who still lives in Harpenden.**

ment because she was very clever but with no place to express this cleverness.'

My sister, Gail, agreed with this assessment. 'She was someone who would read and read and read. When you consider her circumstances she was surprisingly self-educated.'

Sadie was never shy when it came to pushing and promoting her own son. It is important to emphasize that she was never in the game of trying to score points off Eric's own successes, this being the pastime of many mums of the era who flaunted their 'talented' child. Sadie genuinely wanted the best for her only child for *his* sake. She was wide-seeing and wanted him to have at least the chance to improve his lot in life.

Joyce Blacow, née Bennett, another lady who remembers Eric from both school and dance classes, found Sadie a little daunting. 'First of all,' she explains, 'my own mother wouldn't let me speak to Eric, or any of the "rough" boys of the Christie estate. It was a snob thing. This was silly, really, because we were both at the Lancaster Road School. But I used to speak to Eric,' she recalled with a smile, 'because I liked him.'

And Eric liked her, it seemed, as down the years on his occasional excursions to his childhood roots, Joyce would only have to ring and Eric would go over and meet up with her and her husband. I find this particularly interesting about my father: while he was not so bothered about the town and the familiar places of his young days, he was fond of the one-time school chums who had peopled that past. And this remained true throughout his life: where he lived or visited – whether it was Harpenden, Portugal, Florida, or other places – was far less relevant to him than the people he encountered there.

'Sadie was never shy when it came to pushing and promoting her own son.'

Joyce remembers Eric mostly from dancing class. 'But his mother, Sadie, I felt was awfully hard on him,' she recalled. 'She made Eric do what she wanted him to do. She used to stand there overlooking proceedings. Can you imagine this young lad being brought into the all-girl dance school at the bottom of Queen Street in Morecambe, and he'd have to make his entrance with his mother hovering for some time in the background? At least he had separate lessons from our group, which was something, but it wasn't very nice for Eric, who was such a lovely young lad; he really was. All us girls in the class felt sorry for him, because you could tell he personally wasn't the least bothered about being there. But his mother was *very* determined that he made a better life for himself. And of course,' she added, 'who is to say she wasn't right long-term? It served him as training for his later career in show business.'

My mother obviously got to know my father's parents very well over the years. 'Sadie loved it whenever Eric visited,' she said. 'But the problem was, Sadie would never let you get to bed at night. She would keep us up half the night just talking, and in the end – particularly next day – we'd be absolutely

left Eric with son Steven. Steve very quickly grew accustomed to Eric's joking around and would often be his willing straight man!

right Neil Durden-Smith threatens Eric with a live lobster, while his wife, TV presenter Judith Chalmers, has her own lobster problems! Joan Morecambe, the toddler and the man at the left of the photo seem completely unfazed by goings-on.

exhausted. And what she was doing was repeating the same stories over and over again. It was the stories of Eric's whole life from childhood through the touring years. Eventually Eric would give in through tiredness and say, "That's it, I'm off to bed." George would go to bed too. I was too soft. Somehow I allowed her to keep making us endless cups of tea through the night as we carried on with the same stories. The amazing thing was how she would still manage to be up bright and early the following morning as if nothing had happened.'

I know from my personal experience that however repetitive Sadie was she was a gifted speaker who could easily entice you into her world. 'She knew how to tell a story,' agreed my mother, Joan. 'This must partly be where Eric got the gift from.'

Joan's relationship with Sadie and George began when she first became serious with Eric. 'I don't know why, but Sadie was in awe of the fact that my parents owned a hotel in Margate. Eric and I got engaged, which she was thrilled about, and we had the notice put in the local Morecambe paper. Then, a few weeks later, we decided to announce that we were getting married. "We've only just announced the engagement," Sadie said. It was almost as if we were forced into getting married, but we weren't at all. It was more about Eric's

left **At the back, Eric stands next to Roy Castle. In the front, holding the drink, is Myra Secombe (Sir Harry's widow).**

right **Eric standing between former next-door neighbours Alison and Richard.**

work. He had a few days off in December, so we went for it. Plus the fact my mother and family were really obliging and offered us the hotel, which made it all possible.

'Sadie was filled with horror at going to Margate for the wedding and meeting everyone. People didn't travel nearly so much back then, and she also had a slight inferiority complex about it. It was about my family being southerners. That was out of the northern working-class realm in which they existed: the social divide, as it was seen to be. But then within a couple of hours of being down there they loved it and they got along perfectly with my family.'

George enjoyed himself too, but of course George enjoyed most things that made Sadie happy. 'Both Sadie and George loved Westerns,' my mother explained. 'And I think George liked to see a bit of the Hollywood star in himself.'

I remember him as tall, slim and good-looking, with a thin, Ronald Coleman-style moustache. 'It was the likes of John Wayne, Gary Cooper, Glen Ford who influenced them,' said Joan. 'These film characters were almost real for Sadie and George. And George modelled himself a little bit on them.' I find this fascinating, considering George was relatively indifferent when it came to his own son's later stardom.

The usual suspects! Gail and Eric with Joan and Gary – the family Morecambe. Taken on the steps leading down to Eric's original open-plan study, a year or two before it was supplanted by the upstairs spare bedroom which would remain his office for the rest of his life. The 'spare bedroom' became the subject of a Channel 4 documentary in 2004.

'Sadie and I in so many ways were so different, and lived in such a completely different world,' said my mother, 'and yet she came to rely so much on me as a friend. She relied on me to give her all the news on our lives, because she could never get much sense out of Eric, who was a typical young man – very impatient and not bothered about lengthy discussions on the state of everything.'

I certainly recognized, even as a kid, that my grandparents were not sophisticated people – they didn't need to be. But Eric's path in life meant that he *did* need to be, and I had trouble trying to equate his humble background with his starry present.

Watching a programme on David Beckham I felt such empathy on my father's behalf. In Beckham's case, he was the boy-made-good Londoner, who in a relatively short time had become a multi-millionaire sports star whose features would adorn myriad magazines, papers, and merchandise. In his earliest of interviews the wide-eyed lad still talked and behaved in a rough, artless way natural to his upbringing. But, fifteen years on, listen to him now. Look at his deportment and the calm, intelligent way he handles the media. And I believe Eric, if in a less intense way, went through something very similar.

My mother explained to me how little Sadie and George wanted to travel away from Morecambe. 'The only time they loved it was when we did the summer seasons and they would be dropped off at our rented house by their friends and neighbours, Madge and Tom Shaw.'

I heard quite a bit about Madge and Tom from various people still living in Morecambe, and eventually caught up with their son, John, who kindly lent me some photos for this book which are published here for the first time.

As Eric's career progressed, Sadie and George would become less involved with his everyday life. That would become my mother's domain – and it would soon embrace another young entertainment hopeful: a certain Ernest Wiseman.

When Eric Met Ernie

I'm Not All There

I'm not all there, there's something missing

I'm not all there, so folks declare

They call me 'Looby' 'Looby', nothing but a great big 'Booby'

Point and say that's where you want it

But that's just where I've got it

I know they think I'm slow

Let them think, let them think, I don't care

When I go to the races, my fancy to back

If I back a winner, they give me my money back

'Cause I'm not supposed to be all there

Let them think, let them think, I don't mind

Courting couples in the park, on any night you'll find

If you stay, they'll separate, for love's not always blind

But they let me stay and watch them, and they never seem to mind

'Cause I'm not supposed to be all there.

(THE WORDS TO THE SONG THAT ERIC AUDITIONED WITH FOR THE
IMPRESARIO JACK HYLTON)

In his 1990 autobiography, *Still On My Way To Hollywood*, Ernie Wise recalled the first time he set eyes on Eric. 'I first met Eric in the spring of 1939. I was on tour with Jack Hylton, doing a concert at a cinema in Manchester, and all of five months in the business … It was my usual practice … to sit out front

An unusual photo more resembling a gathering of the Krays' clan! On the left is one of their two ATV scriptwriters, Dick Hills. Then comes Ernie and the others must be technicians from the ATV shows. It is possible that the one on the extreme right is their other scriptwriter, Sid Green.

casting an "experienced" eye over the ever-hopeful acts. At this point enter Eric Bartholomew accompanied by his mother, the redoubtable Sadie.

'Eric took the stage and went into a number called "I'm Not All There". This he followed with a very polished impression of Flanagan and Allen. How the hell he did it I don't know! He played each character separately but somehow wove them together in such a way that we were convinced there were two people up there on stage. Everybody was terribly impressed. The Flanagan and Allen brought gasps of admiration and I began to get seriously worried about my future career. I had a lot of push in those days, a hard core, but I have to admit my self-esteem took a bit of a knock from Eric even though we never said a word to each other … '

In looking back at the beginnings of Eric and Ernie's working relationship it is interesting also to consider briefly the beginnings of northern comedy, of which both men were a product.

Northern humour developed mostly in the mill towns. From the start of industrialization until well into the twentieth century most working people in the north of England spent tedious and soul-destroying days toiling in vast spaces in large numbers, and humour and song became the only way they could express themselves, feel a little alive, and generally relieve the monotony of everyday life. No better example of this can be found than the wealth of comedians produced by the industrial heartland of the northwest. This tradition stretches back to Victorian times, but among the great names of comedy of more recent years are Jimmy Clitheroe, Ken Dodd, Tommy Handley, Victoria

left A very young Ernie Wise. It is probably a photo taken by Eric when the two went on holiday together to Guernsey in the 1940s. A long time before T-shirts and designer shorts. As for the shoes…!

centre and right More photos of Ernie in his dapper youth. Locations unknown.

Wood, Stan Laurel, Thora Hird, George Formby, Albert Modley, Al Read, Les Dawson, Sandy Powell, Peter Kay, Jewell and Warriss, Morecambe and Wise, and scores of others. (In passing, Sandy Powell is the only entertainer to whom Eric ever sent a fan letter.)

All made their mark in their time. For Victoria Wood and Peter Kay, that time is right now, but for those who know their British comedy history, the others never seem that far away. The late Les Dawson remains perhaps still the most quotable comedian on mother-in-laws. While his material is now widely viewed as outmoded, a form of comedy done to death in pubs, clubs, and variety theatres over too many decades to remember, the natural humour of his gags, reinforced by his deadpan delivery, still survives and surely always will. 'The wife's mother has been married three times. Her first two died through eating poisoned mushrooms!' (In the comedian Jack Dee the deadpan melancholic embodied by Les Dawson lives on, though the mother-in-law jokes are sacrificed for observations of people in general.)

Those bright lights of the north, and many more like them, illuminated the entertainment industry that was born during the Industrial Revolution and reached its zenith in the first half of the twentieth century. Of course the north of England wasn't the sole purveyor of comedy. The humour served up in the south, particularly London, was and is profound – from Charlie Chaplin to

Ernie looking hardly old enough to smoke … is!

Peter Sellers, from Max Miller to Mike Reid, from Flanagan and Allen to Norman Wisdom, Kenneth Williams, Ben Elton, and Harry Enfield.

It's important to remember that over the decades other regions of the United Kingdom, notably the mining towns and shipyard areas, have also produced great comic entertainers, from Tommy Cooper (Wales) to Billy Connolly (Scotland). But the northwest corner of England has consistently yielded up an astounding plethora of talent.

In the eighty or ninety years after 1780 the population of Britain as a whole nearly tripled and the average income more than doubled. The share of farming fell from under a half of the nation's output to just under a fifth, and the making of textiles and iron moved into steam-driven factories. As a result the north experienced exceptionally rapid growth, with the towns of Liverpool, Manchester, Leeds, and Sheffield becoming teeming cities during the nineteenth century. Such monumental changes had not been fully anticipated and were not fully comprehended at the time.

In the early decades of the twentieth century, with much of Europe and

A rare photo of Ernie having a sly fag. Ernie rarely smoked, though he did go through a phase in his late twenties of smoking a pipe.

Ernie when he was still young and sexy!

America fully industrialized, a comic voice emerged that spoke for the age: Charlie Chaplin in his mocking role of Hitler in *The Great Dictator* and as the Tramp in *Modern Times*. In the former film he makes a long speech as the dictator. This is a small part of it and for us, with the benefit of hindsight, it expresses the fallibility of that era:

Greed has poisoned men's souls – has barricaded the world with hate;
has goose-stepped us into misery and bloodshed.

We have developed speed but we have shut ourselves in:
machinery that gives abundance has left us in want.
Our knowledge has made us cynical,
our cleverness hard and unkind.
We think too much and feel too little:
More than machinery we need humanity;
More than cleverness we need kindness and gentleness.

Without these qualities, life will be violent and all will be lost.

Yet out of it all, with Chaplin's huge impetus, grew British comedy, which has continued to thrive and expand as quickly as our great cities did during the nineteenth century. Today saying you are a stand-up comic working the comedy circuit is as cool as saying you're a rock star. Being a comedian in the last part of the twentieth century and the first part of the twenty-first century has meant elevated status. When I was a child at my first school it was nothing short of an embarrassment, and I kept very quiet about my father's work.

Morecambe and Wise were aware of the tradition of northern comedy in Britain at the time of their coming together, even if they were uncertain of the how and why of it. But they were expansive in their taste and deeply curious about the comedy coming out of America as much as the home-grown comedy they themselves would soon be presenting to the world at large.

'Morecambe and Wise were aware of the tradition of northern comedy in Britain at the time of their coming together.'

Although Ernie saw Eric perform for Bryan Michie and Jack Hylton in Manchester, it wasn't until Eric passed the audition and joined them on the road that he got to know his future partner well.

Ernie, who hailed from East Ardsley, Leeds, began his career in show business by performing with his father in clubs around the region. They were billed as Carson and Kid. But Ernie also did plenty of solo work. An article from the *Morley Observer* of Friday, 18 March 1938 bears the headline: 'Youngsters Are Favourites On Morley Stage'. It goes on to list various young acts appearing in a local talent competition – a sort of regional version of today's TV show *Britain's Got Talent*. Out of around twenty finalists, the list was whittled down to five contestants.

An extract from a book entitled *Morley Entertainers* says of the contest: 'The voting by the audience on ballot papers was close. Each of the runners up

Possibly the earliest photographic recording of Eric using his glasses as a prop.

received an award of half a guinea while an additional prize of a special course in tap dancing, given by the society's ballet mistress, went to Hetty Harris. The first prize of three guineas was awarded to Ernest Wiseman whose comedy song and clever tap dance routine brought the house down.'

Over the next two years Ernie would go on to become a child star, a rise culminating in performances at the London Palladium with the popular comic entertainer of the day Arthur Askey.

'It was the beginning of a friendship which would last another forty-three years.'

Shortly after this success Eric and Ernie found themselves travelling together, though each was still a solo act. They shared digs, even shared a bed, which would gently be nodded to in later years when they put a much-loved

bed routine in their TV shows. Sadie spotted the chemistry and it was she who encouraged them to form a double act.

It was at the Empire Liverpool in August 1941 that Eric and Ernie first performed as the double act Bartholomew and Wiseman. This wasn't a moment that heralded the arrival of a new and wonderful double act – that was still a decade and a half away – but it was the beginning of a friendship and a working partnership which would endure until Eric's death forty-three years later.

Eric and Ernie hadn't been teamed up for very long when they were to see their partnership put on hold. The Second World War began.

Eric's World War

'When the war was on, I went down the mines as a Bevin Boy. My height was no handicap, as I worked lying down. Happy days? Yes, the days were very happy indeed – I was working nights.'

Gordon Jay at around the time he first met Eric as a war-time Bevin Boy.

Gordon and Bunny Jay (brothers whose real name was Jones) were the doyens of British variety bills, appearing in countless pantomime seasons over countless decades, and only recently announced their retirement. Catching up with them face to face was a privilege, but I would be lying if I said there wasn't an ulterior motive to my wanting to interview them. For quite unbelievably it emerged, during a street-corner conversation with Bunny, that not only was his brother down the mines during the war as a Bevin Boy, as Eric was, but that Gordon and my father worked in the same pit and shared the same digs.

There's been a lot in the news lately about the Bevin Boys. They appear to be getting belated recognition for their part in the war effort. As for Bunny, well, to find a Bevin Boy who had come across my father at that time would have been thrilling for me, but to meet one who had not only shared digs with him but also gone into the same profession after the war was genuinely remarkable.

Curiously, just as I set about interviewing Gordon and Bunny, I received an email from someone called Andrew Baird who had managed to track me down. Andrew first met my father as opponents on the football pitch as kids. 'Later, we met just after he was called up as a Bevin Boy,' he recalled. 'Based upon Eric's experience of that, and the advice he gave me, I volunteered for the Royal Navy and went to sea as part of an Atlantic convoy. We were attacked by a German U-Boat and we lost at least one ship. When I relayed my experience to Eric after the war, I made it quite clear that this was the only trouble I experienced during my three years.'

A young Eric, circa 1947, with girlfriend, in a time before his trademark horn-rimmed specs!

The years went by, but Andrew and Eric were destined to meet again. Eric became a director of Luton FC, and Andrew became the bank manager for Mansfield Town FC. 'After the match we had a long, long chat,' says Andrew. 'We agreed to catch up at the return match if your dad was free to get up to it. Well, he was. He strode into the Directors' lounge asking after me, only to be told by the Mansfield Chairman that I was now the banker for Manchester United FC. To be frank, I didn't think Eric would've been free to make it to

Eric with the same girlfriend's family.

that return match. I felt guilty when I learned what had happened. I sent a letter to him care of Luton Town FC, but didn't get a reply. I was not surprised!'

Rest assured, Andrew, Eric would have fully understood, and the lack of a reply would have been a result of the letter not having been passed on to him.

Back to Gordon and Bunny Jay and their memories of Eric during the war years. In 1943 the government had got in a bit of a panic after concluding that Britain was becoming very short of coal. Many of the young miners had either been called up to fight or had transferred to munitions factories where the pay was better. The then Minister for Labour, Ernest Bevin, proposed that a ballot be drawn up conscripting those boys with a certain letter after their name to go down the mines. The proposal was accepted, and these boys were for ever to be known as Bevin Boys.

'The year was 1944,' recalled Gordon Jay. 'Your father and I would both have been eighteen years of age. I remember clearly the first time I saw him. He approached me as all of us new Bevin Boys gathered for our employment for the New Town Colliery, near Manchester. He was wearing a trilby hat and long coat. We sort of knew each other through show business – or at least we did after talking for a few minutes. I think we decided there and then to hang on to each other, because it was fairly evident that we were the only ones in entertainment.'

And it is true that not only was Eric in entertainment at this time, but he had come straight from his full-time employment to help the war effort.

'Being an entertainer then wasn't like it is now. It was still considered, shall we say, unusual.'

'I wasn't due for call up until May 1944,' said Eric in an interview with writer Dennis Holman back in 1972, 'so in the meantime I got a job in ENSA [Entertainments National Service Association, set up in 1939 to provide entertainment for Britain's armed forces during the Second World War] as straight man to a Blackpool comic named Gus Morris. Gus had won the Military Medal in World War I. He had been wounded by a burst of machine gun fire. He couldn't bend his right knee, and his left he could bend only half way, and he had only one eye, but he was a very funny man and very kind to me.

'I remember he and I were at St Helens. The following week we weren't working, so I went home on the Saturday night after the show. On the Monday came a notice in the post for me to report to the labour exchange. I went down there and took my place in the queue.

'"Bartholomew?"

'"Yes."

'"Hullo, Eric, how are you?" said the man whom I knew.

'"Fine," I told him.

'"Matter of fact, the doctor thinks so too. Your medical report says you're A1, and you're one of the chosen few who are going down the mines."'

Gordon Jay then took up the story from the arrival day: 'We tried to get the powers that be to let us stay together in digs, rather than shared rooms on site with everyone else. But they weren't having that. First thing we had to do' – he winced at the memory – 'was have a medical; about twenty of us. We had to strip bollock-naked and line up in front of the MO to be examined. We had lunch in the canteen where we were given a lecture on safety and different things, and we were told we were going down the pit the following afternoon. Afterwards the group broke up, and Eric and I were left hanging around there like a couple of pillocks. I think we were both born cowards and were fairly anxious about the whole set-up in any case. I mean, being an entertainer then wasn't like it is now. It was still considered, shall we say, *unusual*. We were called over, eventually, and told that they'd decided we would be allowed to stay in digs

How Ernie Wiseman and Eric Bartholomew triumphed over adversity and became

MORECAMBE AND WISE

or The Case of the Man with the Short Fat Hairy Legs

by Joan Revill

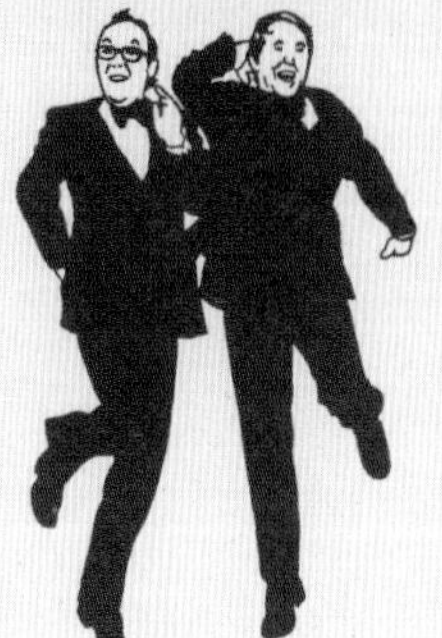

Ernie Wise was on stage first. Leeds, 3 a.m., 27th November 1925. And whether he was drawn by Walt Disney, as alleged in certain quarters, or whether he arrived by the more conventional method, he has a horoscope and that horoscope is *beautiful*. Libra rising in the east, the Sun in Sagittarius. Venus and Jupiter, astrology's two Fortunes, are ascendant ruler and Sun ruler respectively, and are closely conjoined at the nadir of the chart, the inner core of our personality. The looks, the popularity, the sheer lovableness of the man are evident from the word go. Libra and Venus are all charm and sociability. Sagittarius and Jupiter are the best of pals and the luckiest, nicest, cheerfulest, openest and handsomest too! Not only is ruling Venus (representing Ernie personally) thoroughly imbued with the Jovian qualities, but the Sagittarian Sun receives its sole aspect from Jupiter which exaggerates, enriches and expands the ... inherent warmth and

has a sterling character. He is loyal, his affections are steady and sincere, and he takes on responsibilities and duties cheerfully.

Eric's mum will tell you. It was she who started and fostered the double act of Morecambe and Wise. Both lads were juvenile discoveries and she saw at once that ...

never did wrong. Not that he was prim or prissy, or goody-goody, which is a person who justs acts good but is really not good inside. Ernie was just naturally good, naturally truthful, fair and honest . . . Ernie has a genuine purity of heart.'

Eric: He's got short, fat, hairy legs.

Sun Sagittarians do not have short, fat, hairy legs. They have limbs like Greek gods—long, muscular, athletic. Ernie Wise just keeps his concertina'd up so the rest of us poor mortals are not even more suicidally discontented with our lots.

Nevertheless, the character is complex with its easy-going, pleasure-loving Venus/Jupiter set in the austerity of Capricorn and further strengthened by Saturn. Ernie's description of himself as a cautious optimist is probably as good as any. It is Ernie who has always managed the business side of the partnership. (Quote: 'Ernie always enjoys administration and logistics and I let him have his fun.') However, the all-important conjunction although sextile to careful Saturn on one side, is sex- ... Uranus on the

ds fascina-
d the whole
l picture of
its finest

e soil, are
fat, hairy

rine con-
Saturn/
ne, signi-
h. Yet
, Grand
Moon,
Grand
nd the
happily
Water,
r gives
se and

, hairy

our in
m his

Venus
glove
d the
n are
well
uler.
usly
f the
ning
rnie
n is
tuff
na-
ust
ery

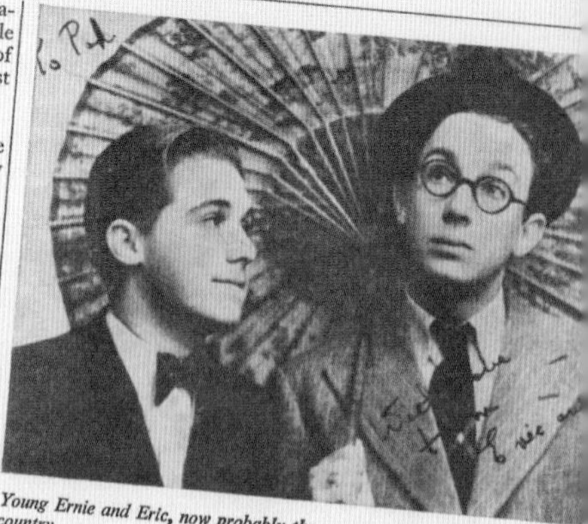

Young Ernie and Eric, now probably the most popular comedy partnership in this country.

Eric: When he was a lad he had a penny a week pocket money, and out of that—he saved.

To continue. Mercury is in its own house, the third, so the mentality is of the highest. It is in Sagittarius giving a great sense of fun. As already remarked, it forms a Grand Trine with the Moon and Neptune. Ladies and gentlemen, if one is asked in the astrological guild examination to name the configuration most likely to lead to a nature of delicate susceptibility, artistic imagination and sloppy sympathy, one says—the Moon, Mercury and Neptune in a Grand Trine, and one is right.

Eric: What are those black lines in your working chart going from marvellous Pluto at the top to Venus and Jupiter up to no good at the bottom?

Opposition which, here, could indicate changes in the career.

Eric: Changes in the career! He hasn't changed his material ... years let alone ...

Ernie's father was a ra... porter who supplemented h... a week by local entertaining... the age of six Ernie was in ... act which blossomed as Carson and his Little Won... That was the Bryan Michie er... the talent contest. The Li... Wonder crushed all rivals and put into Jack Hylton's tour version of *Youth Takes a Bow*. 13 he was famous. It was then met Eric Bartholomew, fr... Morecambe. Although the cros... talk of Carson and Wonder w... highly regarded in the Workin... Men's Clubs of Leeds an... environs, Ernie solo was billed ... 'The Jack Buchanan of Tomor... row' and it was to be a slick song and dance routine along the hig... road of success for him. Joining up with Master Eric meant a diversion to comedy, so his career ... change. And, of ...

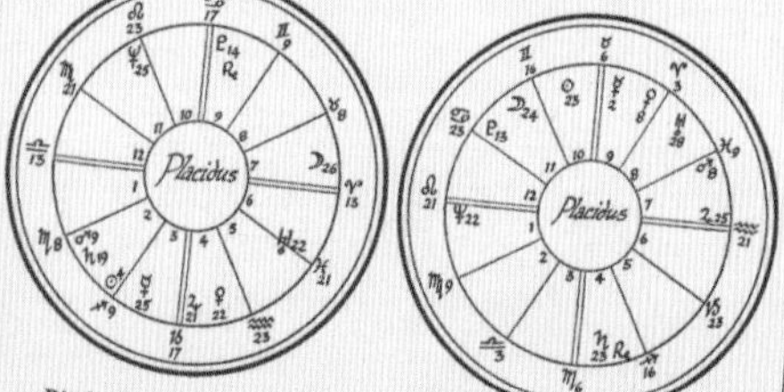

Birth data: Ernie Wise, 3.00 a.m. November 27, 1925 Leeds.

Birth data: Eric Morecambe, 12.00 p.m. (BST) May 14, 1926, Morecambe (Lancs.)

...ribes them. Charmers, showbiz people, glamorous and attractive but not always reliable. Sometimes scandalous, sometimes muddlers, often apt to work very hard in order to escape work. Nomadic, unsettled citizens of our brave new welfare state on the whole.

Eric: That's me folks!

It cannot be denied that Eric ... Neptune rising in Leo in his horoscope which bestows that ... of personality. Well aspected gives a romantic or spiritual ...ure. Poorly aspected, as this is, the prognosis is dubious.

...: Speak it!

...e have had occasion to ... out before that the horo... of those born in the sum... months of the late 1920s and 1930s have a very fair ...e of being dominated by ..., a planet which all agree is ...ary for our development, ...hich no one really wants. ... with many others, Eric ...ambe has it as a 'singleton' ...pio. That is, alone in one ... the zodiac, and as his

partner's lucky Venus/Jupiter conjunction is at the nadir of *his* chart, so Saturn is at the nadir of Eric's. Eric's mother has remarked that they teamed up because they were opposites and, as always, Eric's mother was right.

The centre of Ernie Wise's chart is sweetness and light; the centre of Eric Morecambe's is jitters and apprehension. Ernie's Venus/Jupiter conjunction is well aspected but Eric's Saturn supports an alarming Fixed Square. Saturn opposes the Sun and is in quadrature to Neptune in the east and to Jupiter in the west which, in turn, oppose each other and are then in quadrature (or square) to the Sun.

Eric: Well then (bravely) *what happens?*

For a long while, as likely as not, nothing—at least not on the surface. But these Squares, especially those in Fixed signs, are a pointer to tremendous tension building up inwardly or thunder clouds piling up outwardly, depending on how it takes you. Eric's worked inwardly ...

wardly he was outstand... cessful (although, Erni... us, always incident and ... prone), but inside he is ... assures us) one of the worriers and hypochondria... Getting to the top is not... the strains and stresses imp... staying at the top. Ernie, w... more adaptable nature, ... well. Eric didn't and after d... himself for years and living o... nerves, he had a near fatal ... attack on the night of the 7th November 1968.

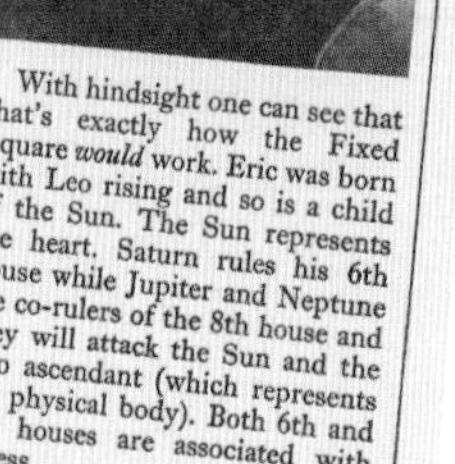

With hindsight one can see that that's exactly how the Fixed Square *would* work. Eric was born with Leo rising and so is a child of the Sun. The Sun represents the heart. Saturn rules his 6th house while Jupiter and Neptune are co-rulers of the 8th house and they will attack the Sun and the Leo ascendant (which represents the physical body). Both 6th and 8th houses are associated with illness.

He had had warnings. Called up as a Bevan boy during the war he was discharged after a year down the pits with heart trouble. With progressions and transits continually touching up the sensitive spots on the Fixed Square he was always liable to some disaster or other, but ...

which floored him in 1968. By Secondary Directions it had moved the fraction necessary to put it exactly midway between natal Sun and Saturn, which is said to pinpoint mental, emotional or physical crises. Added to that, Neptune was in transit through Scorpio and, in 1967/68, was brooding darkly over natal Saturn. Both the symbolically progressed Neptune and the transiting Neptune have moved on

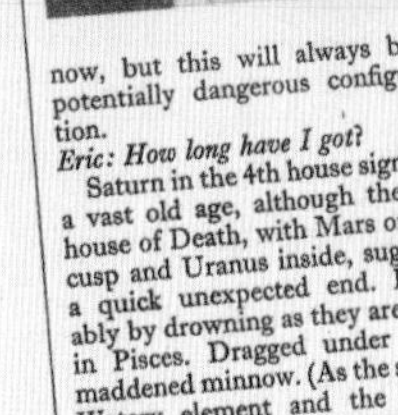

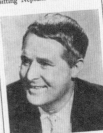

now, but this will always be a potentially dangerous configuration.

Eric: How long have I got?

Saturn in the 4th house signifies a vast old age, although the 8th house of Death, with Mars on the cusp and Uranus inside, suggests a quick unexpected end. Probably by drowning as they are both in Pisces. Dragged under by a maddened minnow. (As the strong Watery element and the rising Neptune show, Eric is a famed fisherman, jeered at by every trout from here to Gravesend.)

Ernie: But is there nothing good? Naturally he can't have such a lovable horoscope as mine, but . . .

Of course there are goodies. In any event, a Fixed Square isn't bad. It's an incentive. The celestial bodies bickering in this way ... equivalent to rubbing two Boy ...

you get a bonfire. Wonderfully ambitious—much more so than Venus and Jupiter. But in the more accepted sense, the Sun is sextile Uranus which is magnetic and provides exceptionally lucky breaks. Mars trines Pluto (as for Ernie) which is record breaking efforts. Jupiter is in the 7th house which produces happy and successful partnerships, both marital and professional. It is in close good aspect to the Geminian Moon for a particularly happy marriage. Sun and Moon, the male and female principles, are harmoniously semi-sextile. In this tender context Venus must be consulted. She is in passionate, impetuous Aries, well supported by Mars, which explains why Eric, despite his Saturnian bias, had a whirlwind courtship and married in December 1952 when the progressed Sun and progressed Moon were conjoined and progressed Venus was at the midheaven. It was poor old Ernie (Venus in Capricorn sextile Saturn) who waited faithfully for seven years. Ernie met Joan in Lord John Sanger's Circus, where they all did a stint soon after the war, but if he had married then, who would have looked after Eric? If the situations had been reversed one fears that selfish Venus-in-Aries Eric wouldn't have cared who was going to look after Ernie! Having got Eric safely provided for, Ernie married a month later when his progressed Moon was back on her natal place in the 7th house and reactivating its natal Grand Trine aspects.

Eric: But what have I got to confound his Libra-rising-Sun-in Sagittarius lark?

You are equally fortunate. Leo rising, ruling Sun in Taurus in the 10th house which is the area of social and business aspirations, fame and honour. Just by looking at the design of the horoscope, all the planets except Saturn are above the horizon which is fine for

all outward bound enterprises.

Eric: And Saturn?

Saturn nags away below the surface, not discernible to the naked eye.

Mercury, right at the midheaven, well aspected to Mars and Jupiter, makes words the *modus operandi* of success. Like the Sun, Mercury is in Taurus, which has a strong sense of humour, especially when tickled by jovial Jupiter.

Ernie: So here we are, the most popular comedians in the country, courted, feted, fawned upon and, of course, loved. What future delights await us?

(That's Venus/Jupiter talking.)

Eric: How much longer can it last?

(That's Saturn.) Well—

Ernie: Only nice things.

Well, Jupiter moves into Tauru... in March 1976 where it will sta... for about a year which should ... a very nice thing indeed for Eri... Otherwise, for both, changes see... to be on the way. Pluto will ... hovering over Ernie's ascenda... from 1976 until the end of t... seventies which brings slow ... drastic remodelling of the envir... ment and life style. For E... 1978/79 finds the progres... ruling Sun in conjunction ... natal Pluto which is more or ... ditto. In the 11th house, tho... it could mean changes in fri... ships but—oh lor!—let's hope... All right Arthur—*now*!

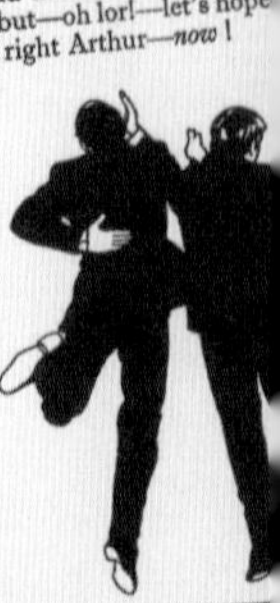

It's always been fashionable and lucrative for superstars to put their names on products while having very little involvement or knowledge of them. While The Morecambe and Wise Joke Book was probably more authentic, the magazine they are fronting would have had very little to do with them.

after all, which was a relief. I think they got the point that as young entertainers we were accustomed to staying in digs as part of our work. Our new digs would be in Salford.'

Their digs were fairly rudimentary, but Gordon doesn't recall this with any rancour – it just was how it was back then. 'We had one room with two iron bedsteads. Eric chose the bed by the window.'

It would be some time later, when Eric was transferred to another mine, that his health rating went from A1 to C3, which, as Gordon pointed out to me, is pretty significant. 'I think he was unlucky because he didn't get the pit he wanted to go on to.' This is true, and he ended up in one that, as Eric himself

A 1950s photo showing Eric flanked by his wife Joan, left of photo, and the singer Alma Cogan. Eric was very fond of Alma and was devastated by her very premature death.

described, 'had seams literally no more than two feet high'.

'We did a month together in digs,' continued Gordon. 'That first day together was a bit frightening. There were a few ashen faces, ours amongst them. Eric and I sat next to each other while the talk went on. The health and safety officer – though I doubt that specific term was used back then – told us we were going down the mine for our first time that afternoon at two o'clock. What's interesting is that they pointed out to us that they couldn't force any of us to go down. But every day we refused to go down added a day to our training. Clever, really, because no one wanted to delay their stay in Manchester, so no one refused to go down.'

So down they went, having been given an upbeat description which explained that the space was such that you could get eight double-decker buses down there, and there were huge air lamps floodlighting the place at all times. 'And it really was the case,' verified Gordon. 'They were very smart, because they took us down to this surprisingly large open space in a cage lift, which moved much slower than you usually would go in one of those things. Soon everyone was down there in this large, well-lit space, and we were given a little explanation about everything, and then we went back up into the daylight. We must have been down there for all of twenty minutes.

'The training then started. We had lectures in the morning, followed by P.E., then boxing. Your dad in boxing gloves and shorts is something I clearly can remember,' chuckled Gordon. 'And then it would be the pit again, though sometimes the timetable would change because of the large number of us that needed organizing.'

Gordon explained that there was a life, albeit a small one, outside of the work. 'On the third day,' he said, 'one of the management girls called us in to tell us they were going to have a social, and asked if we would be willing to do something for it – meaning a routine of some kind. Eric and I looked at each other and shrugged and said, yes, fine – we'll do something. I had my tap shoes with me and some decent clothes and music, so we went away and had a chat about it. After a while Eric looked at me and said, "Do you really want to do this?" I smiled thinly and said, "Not really!" and that was that; we didn't do it. We came up with some excuse the following day that we couldn't find the venue.'

'Eric I found always wanted to talk about his mum and dad. He clearly thought the world of them: he worshipped them.'

As time went on, Gordon explains how the two of them would burn the midnight oil talking about what they would do when they got out of the mines and the war was over. 'It was the only time we could really chat, because when we got to the pit each day we split up. He had a mining mate and I had a mining mate. The strange thing was, we never worked properly as such. We would go down the mines but just to learn things as a way of training for later on.

'But during the hours when we were back on our beds in the digs, we'd chat. Eric I found always wanted to talk about his mum and dad. He clearly thought the world of them: he worshipped them. He was always pondering on what they would have been doing that day, and what they would have had to eat. And if Bunny's and my mother visited, he was straight over to her making a fuss of her. We would walk along the street separately, because Eric would be with our mother, and he would change sides if necessary to make sure he was nearer the road so as to protect her. He was very gentlemanly.'

'I would meet up with Gordon and Eric with my mother at the weekends in

Manchester,' chipped in Bunny. 'We would go to the cinema. I remember one film we saw was Eddie Cantor in *Show Business.*'

I found this very interesting, because from the recollections of his early peers we have already seen that he would spend time watching films whenever he could, particularly at the Saturday morning club in Morecambe that he attended with his chums. And I also knew my father was an Eddie Cantor fan. When I was about six he bought me a Cantor LP, which I adored, and I would go to my local school talking about Eddie Cantor and others of that ilk, wondering why they hadn't heard of him and could only talk about singers called Elvis Presley and the Beatles, of whom I knew just about zilch.

'The rationing was on, of course, but the landlady fed us well,' continued Gordon, recalling the digs he shared with Eric. 'The arrangement was, she gave us a cooked breakfast, packed lunch, and a meal when we came in.'

'We both sensed that if this was what was on offer, then we were going to do all right once we got back on the showbiz road again.'

The first day came and they arrived at the pit to face the usual lecture from a health and safety officer (some things haven't changed). 'Then we were given a pep talk before we went down,' said Gordon. 'Then we had a lunch break and ate our sandwiches, which was always to be a choice of jam or fish paste. A staple diet for the next month. And your dad and me really weren't into that as a diet. In the end we'd drop these sandwiches over someone's fence near the bus stop and nip into a canteen.'

Gordon also remembered other moments spent away from the pits. 'We would go to various theatres, like the Salford Hippodrome, to watch what were without question pretty shoddy revues. They weren't even "tits 'n' tinsel" – this was before those times. I'm not sure what your dad thought of it all. Although it possibly remained unspoken, I think we both sensed that if this was what was on offer, then we were going to do all right once we got back on the showbiz road again.'

And the theatres and cinemas themselves?

'Gone!' said Gordon without a shred of doubt. 'It was a different world.'

What still remains are some of the public houses of that time, yet Gordon was quick to tell me, 'I can't remember a single occasion I went to the pub with your dad, which I find strange. We were all young and keen to get out to have our beers and fags and be a part of the adult scene. But your dad never did.'

What Gordon said doesn't strike me as totally surprising. My father once told me that he never even had alcohol in the house until he was in his late thirties. It was considered a luxury, or something the privileged classes would do – but not someone from his background. Also, he was never keen on going to pubs: partly this was because he was so recognizable, but as well as that he just didn't particularly enjoy them. On top of that he had never been a beer drinker, which was the chosen drink of the working class. 'When I reached my thirties and the M and W shows were starting to happen for us,' he said, '*then* I started bringing drink home and we had a drinks cabinet and so on. But even then, it was probably limited to a whisky on a Saturday night.'

When my family moved home in 1968, the drinks cabinet began to have more frequent use for my father, who never really had a major problem with alcohol yet seemed on occasion to be making up for its paucity in previous decades. My sister Gail later inherited the cabinet, but by then my father had a walk-in bar in the living room and it remains well stocked to this day. Indeed during a very recent examination I discovered many bottles of spirits still standing on shelves as he had left them anything from twenty-five to forty years ago.

It was time to move on from the training colliery. 'But Eric was disappointed because he didn't get the colliery he wanted to move to,' explained Gordon. 'I was as pleased as punch because I got the one I wanted. I'm not sure what Eric's next mine was like.'

Awful! This I concluded long ago, on the basis that my father came out of the mines with a health rating of C3. He was sent home to his parents, spending the next six months recuperating and the rest of his life bemoaning his days as a Bevin Boy.

'We never exchanged addresses,' said Gordon. 'You would do in this day and age, but with the war on it all somehow seemed less relevant. Nowadays, of course, you'd just exchange mobile numbers or email addresses. I don't think my parents even had a telephone at home back then. So we more or less shook hands, and with a "Cheerio!" and "Good luck!" walked off in our separate directions.

'I often wondered if the gang we were together with doing the mining era ever realized who this young lad became. Probably not. It's not the most obvious connection, and he worked under a different name soon after the war.'

Gordon wasn't even sure himself how he made the connection between the young lad he had befriended in the pits and the comic icon Eric Morecambe. 'It's annoying, really. I can't recall a definitive moment where I suddenly linked the two names. All these years on it just feels like it was something I've always known.'

'My father came out of the mines with a health rating of C3. He spent the rest of his life bemoaning his days as a Bevin boy.'

But that wasn't to be the end of Gordon's association with Eric. When finally they reunited, Eric Bartholomew had by now transmogrified into Britain's leading comedian, Eric Morecambe.

'This reunion was obviously many years later and in very different circumstances,' reminisced Gordon. 'Bunny and I of course followed their double act, as everyone in the business was at some point being compared to Eric and Ernie.'

'Strangely enough,' said Bunny, 'we got to know almost all the other double acts really well, except for Eric and Ernie.'

'Particularly Jimmy Jewell and Ben Warriss,' said Gordon. 'They were the tops post-war, and then Eric and Ernie slowly took over.

'We saw [Morecambe and Wise] at the Lyceum in Sheffield in the mid-fifties. They would have been on a Stan Stennett bill, I imagine. Then in 1961 we were in Bradford with Tommy Cooper doing *Puss in Boots*. Business was crap because there was an outbreak of smallpox, so hardly anyone was venturing outside their front door.

'Tommy became a good mate, but was completely nuts even back then. He wasn't supping in those days – not until after the show! At the same time, Eric and Ernie were performing at the Grand, Leeds, with David Whitfield in

Sleeping Beauty. It was the big, big production that had prior to this been at the London Palladium with Bruce Forsyth and Ted Hockeridge. Tommy said, "I think we should all go over to Leeds to see the lads."' (This is easy to imagine as Eric and Ernie shared a lifelong friendship with the great comedian of the non-magical trick.) '"You can pick me up and drive us there," said Tommy, who I should mention would affectionately call me "My favourite long-nosed git".

'Me and Bunny got chatting with them after the show, and we realized neither of us had a matinée the following day, so we suggested they came over to Bradford for lunch. But the point of all this is that I still hadn't told your father that I was the lad from the Bevin Boy days!

'Everyone in the business was at some point being compared to Eric and Ernie.'

'I went to the hotel to collect Tommy the following morning, and he came down the stairs looking like the wrath of God. The bar must have closed late the previous night! Meantime Eric has arrived at the theatre and gone to the dressing room and is just looking at the props. Bunny and I were playing Hurdy and Gurdy in *Puss in Boots,* which Eric and Ernie had played some years before while working with Harry Secombe at Coventry. And we were just chatting when Eric said, "I'm sure I've seen you somewhere before." So I let on where it was.'

Bunny picked up the story, saying, 'And I walked in to find the two of them in convulsions, and doing the reminiscing thing.'

'Mind you, Eric had a go at me for not saying anything the day before,' Gordon pointed out. 'But you know, people can change and you don't like to go blithering on. Also, you think they might have forgotten, and so you are avoiding that possibility. But we had a great time and talked about catching up another time soon, etc. – and we never saw each other again!'

In parting, Gordon made a point of saying something that I've long said: 'When you watch Morecambe and Wise now and you closely study Ernie, you

realize what a bloody good feed he was for your father. But it's the comedian who gets the laugh and the feed can get overlooked.'

I'm not sure the public understand the purpose of the feed, or straight man, if you prefer. I'm not sure the media do either. Maybe Ernie had the right idea in just accepting it. At least he got half the fame and half the money – even half the awards. It must have irritated at some moments, though. Probably around 3 a.m., when you find yourself wide awake sensing something is niggling you, but not quite sure what!

Their scriptwriter during Morecambe and Wise's halcyon days at the BBC, Eddie Braben, said in an interview that 'even today I don't think we realize just how important Ernie was. I wrote a line once that has often been used since, and Eric said it was so right. He said it was absolutely spot on. They were doing a stand-up and Ernie had to go off quickly for a prop and Eric said, "Don't be long; when you're not here I feel a cold draught all down one side."

'Eric didn't like standing on his own. He didn't like performing on his own. He was OK for a couple of minutes then he'd start to feel uncomfortable.'

Goodbye Theatreland, Hello TV

'Between you and me, I don't really mean all those insults I hurl at Des O'Connor. I think he's one of the greatest singers in the country. He just struggles when he sings in the town, that's all. Have you heard his latest record, Songs for Deaf Lovers? There's a government health warning on every cover.'

The forties and fifties had been Eric's bread-and-butter years before the jam arrived in the sixties in the shape of television. Most achievement in the earlier decades was through radio shows and theatre work, as mentioned in the previous chapter, but TV had lurked there, albeit in the form of appearances on other people's shows, or through their own first BBC series in 1954, *Running Wild*, which seemed to have people running scared!

Below is a wonderful article from that year, published in the weekly magazine *TV Mirror*, about Eric and Ernie's this failed series before it had aired for the first time. What interests me beyond the fact that *Running Wild* nearly finished their careers is that the writer of the piece – like the public at large – didn't really know much about them and had to use physical descriptions to help him. Very different from twenty years later, when they were arguably the most famous faces in Britain.

Eric bringing 'comfort' to Des O'Connor while the singer is recovering in hospital following leg surgery. I remember Eric joking afterwards that Des had been forced in to have his voice removed!

The Lads Who've Got Nothing To Lose
An Article published in *TV Mirror*

Morecambe and Wise, the young comedians from the north, have gained a big reputation on radio. Tonight they begin a new comedy series on TV.

Ever since it was announced that a new fortnightly comedy series starring Morecambe and Wise was starting, the two bright lads from the North have been receiving good advice from their colleagues and friends.

'You keep off TV – it'll do you no good,' was the general burden of their advice.

But Eric Bartholomew, who comes from Morecambe (hence the name), and Ernie Wiseman, who claims Leeds as his native town, think differently. After no fewer than forty-five appearances in *Variety Fanfare*, and their own weekly variety series *You're Only Young Once*, they have no doubts about the power of sound radio to help an artist on his way.

And whatever the dismal Johnnies may say about the dangers of a TV series that gets panned by the critics – well, Morecambe and Wise just aren't worrying.

'The way we look at it is this,' said Morecambe (he is the tall one with glasses), 'TV has come to stay and we've been given our big opportunity. We'd be daft if we didn't take it with both hands. You see, we've got everything to gain and nothing to lose.'

'It isn't as though we were at the end of our careers,' added Wise (the small one with the fair hair). 'You're only young once, that's quite true. But we're young now, both of us. I'm 28 and Eric is 27. And I'd say we've got a few years to go yet.' ↝

A radio series too

'If the public don't like us on Wednesday, that's just too bad. But it won't mean we're finished. Why, we've hardly started yet!'

'And there's another radio series starting in May to keep the wolf from the door,' said Morecambe.

'Not that we're going to flop,' put in Wise, touching wood and stroking the nearest black cat. 'We've had our TV flop already, years ago, in – what was the show called, Eric?'

'Shh!' said Morecambe, quickly. 'You know we never talk about that one. Still, there was one good thing about it. Our producer on that occasion was good old Bryan Sears' – here they fell to their knees and touched their foreheads to the ground – 'and it's Bryan who's going to put us across in this new series.'

I tried to find out something about the new show.

The two boys looked at each other, scratched their hair and seemed a little embarrassed. 'Well, it's a comedy show – we know that much. And it's a revue – there's no harm in telling you that. But as for what it's going to be – look, why don't you watch it and find out?'

'That's what we're going to do,' said Morecambe, changing the subject.

Forty-five 'Fanfares'

Bryan seems a lucky name in the story of Morecambe and Wise. It was another well known Bryan – Michie this time – who first discovered the pair at a juvenile talent contest. That was in 1939, when Eric and Ernie were in their very early teens.

Two years later they were touring with Bryan Michie in his road show. In 1943 they went into *Strike a New Note* at the Prince of Wales Theatre in London – with that great comedian Sid Field.

That's where they were when calling-up time came. Ernie went off with the Merchant Navy; Eric went down the mine, surely the only west-end comedian to become a Bevin Boy.

The war over, back they came to the halls, touring here, there and everywhere – and only just out of their teens! Then came a broadcast from Manchester in *Variety Fanfare*. And another. More followed. Finally they notched up that record of forty-five *Fanfare* appearances since the end of 1951.

'But you'd better not put that in,' advised Morecambe, 'we've always depended on the fact that Ronnie Taylor, the producer, can't count. If he reads that, he won't book us again.'

When I could get them talking seriously I got some pretty definite opinions out of Morecambe about this new TV series. 'It's like this,' he said. 'No one, with the possible exception of Arthur Askey, has yet managed to bring off a TV series with any real success.

'Now don't imagine that we're comparing ourselves with Askey – we don't wear the same size in combs. But we're prepared to look on TV as a completely different medium. We're ready to change our approach and our styles as much as is wanted.'

It is my opinion that they will be a big success. ◆

The writer of the article probably came to doubt his own opinion thereafter.

In the fifties the trials and tribulations that would ultimately lead to a staggering television career were still some years off. In fact so uncertain was the future of what would become Britain's most popular double act, and work of any performing kind so scarce around 1950, that, it has come to light, Ernie wrote to Eric to end the partnership. I have known about this incident since the seventies, when my father, with a reflective chuckle at the fact that it never happened and they had gone on to immense success, one day chose to tell me all about it. What I had *not* realized was that Ernie's letter still existed. I had never seen it until my mother showed it to me while I was working on this book. So fascinated am I by the letter that I persuaded her to allow me to publish it. What strikes me most is the great dignity Ernie retains. Beautifully written with integrity, it expresses warm wishes and the desire to continue their great friendship outside the partnership.

This is the letter in its entirety:

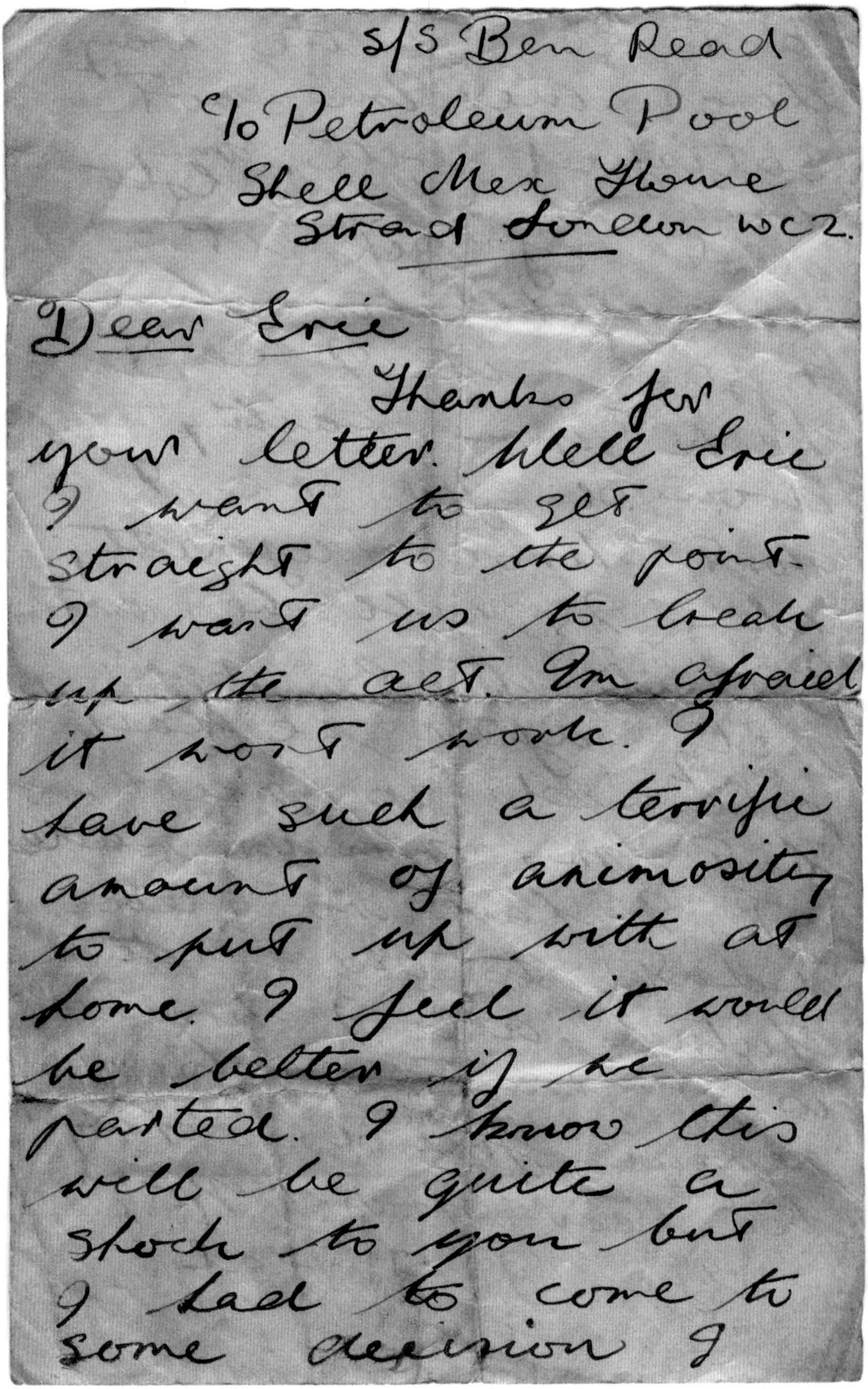

s/s Ben Read
c/o Petroleum Pool
Shell Mex House
Strand London WC2.

Dear Eric

Thanks for
your letter. Well Eric
I want to get
straight to the point.
I want us to break
up the act. I'm afraid
it wont work. I
have such a terrific
amount of animosity
to put up with at
home. I feel it would
be better if we
parted. I know this
will be quite a
shock to you but
I had to come to
some decision I

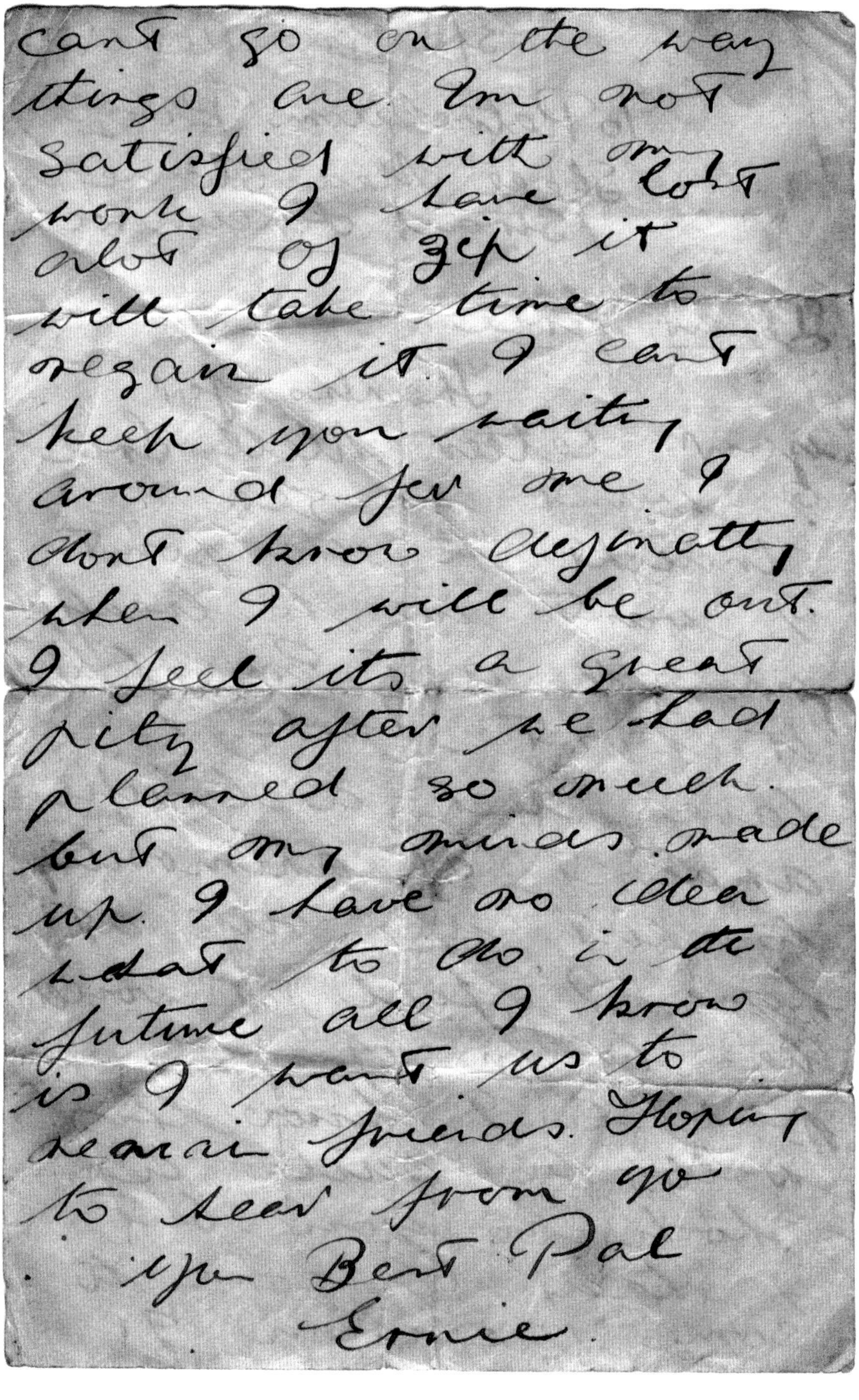

cant go on the way
things are Im not
satisfied with my
work I have lost
alot of zip it
will take time to
regain it I cant
keep you waiting
around for me I
dont know definetly
when I will be out.
I feel its a great
pity after we had
planned so much.
but my minds made
up. I have no idea
what to do in the
future all I know
is I want us to
remain friends. Hoping
to hear from you
your Best Pal
Ernie.

My father's response, he told me, was to write straight back basically saying he'd never heard such rubbish in his life and that Ernie should have a few days' rest to get over it and then they should get back to finding some work – which essentially is what happened.

For me the world of theatre conjures up many images, some of which no doubt can be traced back to the conversations I had with my father throughout my childhood and the hours I spent in those times hanging around theatres and dressing rooms. Eric genuinely loved that era – even the struggle that went with it. 'I would do everything the same only quicker!' he once told me, and it is a line that amused not only me but my own children when I repeated it to them. Though he said it half in jest, I find myself wondering how he could have done any of it quicker – he moved like greased lightning as it was. Harry Secombe said Eric had a quicksilver brain and even nicknamed him 'Quicksilver'. Incidentally, many years before that his mother used to call him 'Jifflearse', a name which is meaningless in the strictest sense yet suggests someone restless and always on the go. This was a total Sadie creation, a word that for her – and me, I should add – conjured an image of someone who can't sit still for a moment, 'jiffle' being similar to 'jiggle', as in 'jiggle about', and 'arse', well . . .

Talking of theatres, Ernie recalled, 'Some of the funniest things happen backstage in the theatre business. We were appearing at a tiny theatre in a very out-of-the-way town. The theatre was old, and the lighting equipment was even older. We asked the electrician backstage to throw the main switch of all the lights in the theatre as a pay-off line to a comedy sketch we were doing at the time. We wanted the whole theatre darkened for just one minute.

'On the first night of the show, we checked with him that he knew exactly when to throw the switch and he nodded that he fully understood. But we were worried, for he was wearing huge rubber boots and thick rubber gloves.

'When the time came for him to throw the switch there was a terrific blue flash and the little electrician was hurled almost from one side of the wings to the other.

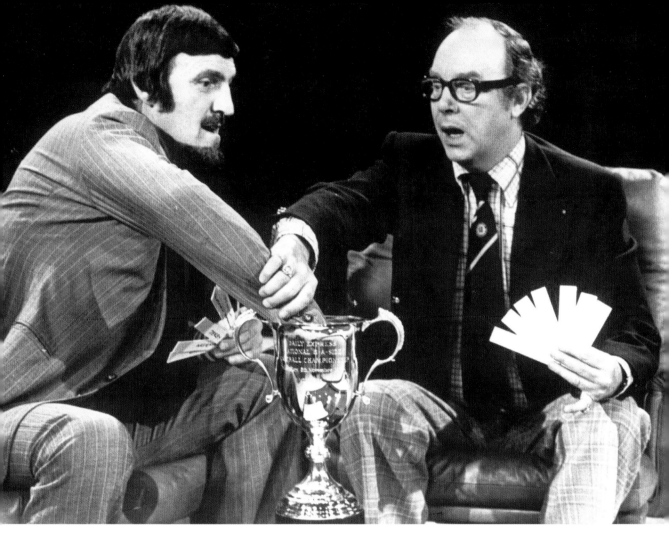

'We rushed to pick him up for fear he might have been electrocuted. "Are you all right?" we asked anxiously. "What happened?"

'"Nothing," replied the charred prostrate little man taking off one of his rubber gloves. "It happens every time I throw that switch!"'

And Eric recalled a time in 1960 when they were working the theatres. 'A cousin [of mine], a rather irresponsible lad with a natural ability to upset other people, asked us if we could get him holiday digs using our names to help him obtain some very pleasant accommodation.

'Naturally we used some influence and fixed up a hotel in Torquay. After a week we had a letter from him saying he was fed up because he had been thrown out of the place. The proprietor had had enough of his practical jokes. He asked us to help him again.

Eric messing around with former football presenter Jimmy Hill. Eric and Jimmy worked together for a charity called the Goal-diggers. Singer Elton John was also part of the team.

left The author with Jimmy
Saville 1984. It was at that
dinner that Jimmy told me
people like Eric should never die.
It's inconceivable that there
comes a time when they're no
longer there.

above Eric with Jimmy Saville
about ten years earlier.

top left **Eric and Ernie with the third member of their double act, the talented, indomitable Ann Hamilton. Straight woman and all round good sport, she became a fundamental part of their seventies shows. It became a passion of Eric's to try to make her corpse, but it very rarely, if ever, happened.**

top right **The wonderful Dame Diana Rigg in a still from her Morecambe and Wise Christmas show appearance 1973. Her dance appearance with Eric and Ernie, as Nell Gynne, was filmed at Broughton Castle.**

left **Glenda Jackson flanked by the boys in what has become one of their best-loved and most remembered sketches – Cleopatra. Interestingly, and the same applies to arguably their best-loved sketch of making breakfast to the music of 'The Stripper', this was not part of a Christmas special. Both famous sketches went out on standard Morecambe and Wise shows from their series.**

Thames TV circa 1982, and he people behind the show. Eric and Ernie are sat in the centre of the front row. On the far left is Derrick Guyler, a variety-hall actor with whom Eric and Ernie had worked on radio in the 1940s. Back then, Derrick had been the star! Next to Derrick is Eddie Braben, Eric and Ernie's scriptwriter. Sat next to the stars themselves is guest actress Hannah Gordon and their long-time producer John Ammonds.

'We managed to fix him some accommodation in Exmouth. Everything was quiet for a few days then another letter arrived. The same thing had happened. He was out, and he wanted help.

'We were tired by this time. But we thought we'd do our best for him just once more. We secured a room for him at Weymouth, and wrote back warning him we had tolerated his troubles long enough.

'For a few weeks all was calm then we received a telephone call: "I'm thrown out again, and I'm mad!" he said. "You ought to get in touch with these proprietors. Tell them, how dare they do this to *You*!"'

Eric and Ernie would keep in touch with theatre work even after the 'jam' had arrived and they no longer really needed panto and summer season. Once they were regular fixtures on television, and this was evident around 1962, they continued the theatre seasons more out of habit than need. It was a habit which lasted right up to Eric's heart attack in November 1968, which would signal the end of many things – including winter and summer seasons – but also the beginning of their television superstardom.

If they thought they were stars in the sixties, then the seventies would show them just how far they could still go.

Heroes and Villains

ERIC: *... Remember how we copied Abbott and Costello when we started? How we liked Laurel and Hardy, and Jewell and Warriss?*

ERNIE: *We must be a mixture of all of them. Yet, pal, we've found our own style as entertainers. We lean on each other.*

ERIC: *Is that what it is? I thought you were drunk ...*

J ust as comics today explain how they have been influenced by Morecambe and Wise – and, believe me, I've come across many and only a few are in double acts – my father was just as influenced by his own heroes. I think his taste in comedy fell into two categories – the comedians who influenced him at the outset and those who influenced him when he was firmly established.

Although it is true that Abbot and Costello were both Eric and Ernie's earliest influence, it was above all Laurel and Hardy who shaped their act. Certainly they were very important for my father: not only he did he tell me so, but you can see it in their work. What fascinates me is that he discovered Laurel and Hardy when still only in his teens, and was still just as big a fan in his fifties. However, as stand-up comedian and sit-com star Lee Mack says, 'If you don't get Laurel and Hardy then you might as well say you don't like comedy full stop.'

Stan Laurel, christened Arthur Stanley Jefferson, was born on 16 June 1890 in Ulverston, at that time in Lancashire but now in Cumbria, about ten miles as the crow flies from Morecambe, where Eric would come into the world thirty-six years later.

Oliver Hardy was born Norvell Hardy on 18 January 1892 in Harlem, Georgia. As a young man 'Babe', as he was also known, had been looking for a career in the military but a love for films made him open a movie theatre in Milledgeville in his home state. This led to his finding work as an actor in Jacksonville, Florida, the home of the Lubin Film Company. Hardy later moved to Hollywood, where he worked as an all-purpose comic at the Hal Roach Studios.

Laurel and Hardy's partnership at Roach began in 1926 – the year Eric Morecambe was born – and within a year of their first joint screen venture they were being announced as a new comedy team.

Laurel and Hardy were a profound influence on Morecambe and Wise not only as comic performers, but also as song and dance men.

When he started out in comedy Laurel was much more of a fall-about comic than he would later become after teaming up with Hardy. It is fascinating to learn that Laurel's earliest working relationship was with Charlie Chaplin, who has, since his death in 1977, been accused (if only in print and by independent observers) of plagiarism. The story goes that much of the concept of Chaplin's huge universally acclaimed screen character the Tramp was actually Stan Laurel's. Laurel, a very gentle man by all accounts, was fully aware of having had his brilliant idea 'stolen' – and apparently it wasn't the first or last time with Chaplin – yet Laurel never stopped thinking, and saying to anyone who would listen, that Chaplin was the greatest comedian there had ever been.

Curiously, and significantly, Chaplin never made a single reference to Stan Laurel in his autobiography, an almost impossible feat when one thinks of their shared history, which included the early years spent on tour together for Fred Karno before the First World War.

Eric rightly claimed that Laurel and Hardy were an inspiration to any double act as they took the 'fat man, thin man' and 'idiot and bigger idiot' concepts to new levels. But Chaplin he disliked passionately. Chaplin, he felt, benefited greatly from the fact that his films were silent and therefore solely dependent on visual content, or pantomime, and to work at their best they needed to be screened at a greater speed than real time, because on screen anyone seen moving faster than people move in reality is straightaway more humorous.

However, when I caught up with comedian and silent-comedy aficionado Paul Merton, he suggested a different explanation as to why Eric hadn't fallen for Chaplin's comic wizardry. 'Your dad's first sight of Chaplin films would have been the Saturday morning pictures at his local theatre, I imagine,' he said. 'At that time – probably mid-thirties – they re-released some Keystone films with Chaplin that were shown at the wrong speed. They were shot at sixteen frames a second and shown at twenty-four, and with a crap musical score thrown on to them, so I don't think people watching them at that time would have a very positive view of Charlie Chaplin.' He added, 'I know Eric Sykes in his autobiography complained of a similar disliking for Chaplin that matches your father's observation. If you see Chaplin as he should be seen it is a very different experience.'

Lee Mack adds: 'As a lad I simply regarded Chaplin as the king of silent comedy. Growing up in an era when video first came in, we were able to appreciate such talents in our own homes.'

One thing with Chaplin is that, unlike Laurel and Hardy, he was unable to make the transfer from silent pictures to the talkies; at least as far as his Tramp was concerned. Eric once wrote, 'In my line of profession Laurel and Hardy feature very highly in my admiration. I never had much time for Charlie Chaplin, although I would not deny he was probably a genius. But to me he wasn't as funny as Buster Keaton. But he must have been a better businessman, because he made and protected a lot more money than most at that time. Harold Lloyd was a marvellous actor-comic and one of the few who successfully made the transition from the silent movies into sound. That is quite an achievement when you consider people such as Jimmy James, Sid Field, Dave Morris and others of that ilk who found it very difficult to perform even on the radio.'

As the above quote makes clear, if Chaplin left Eric a bit cold, Keaton ignited his enthusiasm. At our family home during my childhood and youth, pictures of Buster Keaton lined the hallway and in my father's office there was a sketch, imprinted on a mirror, of Keaton in classic morose pose beneath a boater at the peak of his movie career. This had been a Christmas present from his nephew, Clive, which he really cherished.

'Eric rightly claimed that Laurel and Hardy were an inspiration to any double act.'

Paul Merton went on to make a connection between Eric and Keaton. 'Much of [Morecambe and Wise's] way of performing would have come from the vast wealth of experience of stage work they'd had down the years,' he said. 'And Eric was such a physical comic. They were appearing on a *Royal Variety Show* at the London Palladium, and Eric does this great leap from one staircase to another at the back of the set, and then is having to do pratfalls in the same routine. Very, very physical stuff and brilliant. He was a great faller; an adroit physical comic, and you can't help but wonder if, in view of his love of some of the silent comedians, there was some inspiration from Buster Keaton there.'

By the end of his life Keaton had advanced the art of film-making through his superb writing and direction, and he had developed unique camera innovations unsurpassed even today. He is universally acclaimed as a genius; certainly Eric Morecambe would have gone along with that. Groucho Marx was of the opinion that Chaplin was the funnier of the two, but that Keaton made greater films.

And there, perhaps, is the truth, if truth is to be found in what is ultimately a subjective issue.

I find the stories of Keaton's life as fascinating as his work. When he was only around three years of age he caught his right forefinger in a clothes wringer, losing the first joint, gashed his head near the eye with a brick that ricocheted after he threw it at a peach tree, and was sucked out of an upstairs window by a passing cyclone that carried him floating through the air and deposited him, fortunately unhurt, in the middle of a street a few blocks away. No wonder he became an expert at taking heavy falls in his stage act with his parents.

Harold Lloyd was one of Eric's biggest heroes. I recall afternoons of reruns of Lloyd on TV, me and my father sitting on the sofa, him smoking his pipe and falling about laughing. For him the most appealing part of Lloyd's comedy was his abundant energy and sincerity: he seemed to do so much without any affec-

Interesting that comedian and presenter Paul Merton sees Lloyd as having had an influence on Eric's work, because in this the most famous of all Lloyd's comic sequences he even looks like a young Eric Morecambe.

tation or obvious effort – which is similar to the illusion Eric and Ernie themselves created. The harder the rehearsals and the greater the general effort put into each *Morecambe and Wise Show*, the easier and less complicated the final result appeared. The obvious analogy is of the duck serenely moving across the water's surface while beneath the surface it's paddling like crazy. That's how the illusion always worked for Morecambe and Wise, and how it clearly worked for Harold Lloyd.

By the mid-sixties Eric was in search of a new direction, away from the stereotypical, hapless funny man and towards a much sharper, wittier comedy character, and here the most important influences were two American performers: the evergreen Groucho Marx and Phil Silvers.

Julius Henry Marx (Groucho) is generally agreed to be the most popular and widely recognized of all the Marx Brothers owing to his outrageous on-screen insults and one-liners, which are as strong and as effective today as when first filmed. His screen character was always that of a wise-cracking, cigar-toting, middle-aged man with wire glasses and a big black moustache. One of the reasons I know Eric adored him so much was because Groucho had such wonderfully eccentric notions. Eric's favourite was that Groucho wanted, whenever on screen in a Marx Brothers movie, to wear a painted moustache. There was never any explanation as to why, but the effect was certainly distinctive. According to an interview with Groucho, the producers didn't want him to have a painted moustache, but he just turned up with it anyway.

'Everything comes harder,' Groucho said about ageing during a serious interview with his biographer Charlotte Chandler in the seventies. 'You have to concentrate to do what you didn't have to think about before. You can't take things for granted. You can't even take salt for granted.' Groucho ended that particular interview by saying, 'I'm still alive. That's about it.'

And this reminds me of my father just two weeks before his death. We were having lunch together in a London hotel restaurant and despite being just fifty-seven he was bemoaning the woes of ageing. 'You know you're getting older when it takes half an hour in the bathroom every morning to do what used to take five or ten minutes. And then you find you have all these wild nasal hairs and rogue eyebrows shooting off at tangents that never used to need sorting out: they just were never there before.'

It was Groucho at his zenith – the Groucho of the thirties Marx Brothers movies – that Eric turned to when looking to incorporate something else into his own comic persona. As well as being inspired by the man's cheekiness and imposing screen presence, Eric, with the help of his and Ernie's producer John

Ammonds, took the skip-dance that Groucho created in one of his films and modified it into the outro of each of their shows after they had sung 'Bring Me Sunshine'. It remains perhaps the most vivid signature of Morecambe and Wise even today. I would go so far as to say it has become a symbol of seventies British light entertainment – the era of flared suits, gaudy colours, and politically incorrect gags. This image of Eric skipping away has adorned at least four biographies of Morecambe and Wise and a book of short stories of mine, was the basis of the poster for the West End tribute play *The Play What I Wrote*, and has been emulated in television ads such as those made for Marks & Spencer a few years ago and one shown in 2008 for a bedding company. Comic Relief also used the image in 2009 for their charity. Giant posters abounded showing Lenny Henry in the skip-dance pose, while wearing an Eric and Ernie T-shirt depicting the comics with red noses. It even appears throughout this book. And, to top it all, Sue Barker and John McEnroe emulated it to the sound of Eric and Ernie singing 'Bring Me Sunshine' as the two tennis presenters skipped across the rainswept Centre Court at Wimbledon. I can't imagine what Eric and Ernie would have made of all the fuss. They'd have been thrilled on one hand, no doubt, and utterly perplexed on the other.

The final piece in the creation of the BBC model of Eric Morecambe owed much to another great American comedy hero, Phil Silvers, who was born on 11 May 1911. The comic actor's best-known work, and the one which influenced Eric, was *The Phil Silvers Show* aka *Bilko!,* in which Silvers played Sergeant Ernest G. Bilko. The plots were always inventive, the supporting cast sharp, and the scenes dominated by Silvers and his snappy comedy repartee. What Eric mostly admired was the way he had created this character that could devastate with a single line, and yet be the most charming person on the planet if it allowed him to get his own way. There is no better example of this in *The Morecambe and Wise Show* than when Eric confronts a guest star, one moment displaying utter charm and respect, the next being outrageously rude. A good example was when Alec Guinness walks up to them:

Eric (confidentially to Ernie): Watch out! There's a drunk come on.

Or when the renowned opera singer John Hanson bursts into song:

Eric: Get off! We don't want that rubbish here.

And there were many more, all pure Phil Silvers in terms of delivery and technique.

'Eric took the skip-dance that Groucho created in one of his films and modified it into the outro of each of their shows.'

One final hero I should mention in passing, and who had absolutely nothing to do with comedy, was the late, great jazz musician Duke Ellington. Eric recalled how he came close to meeting his idol.

'I was working in a theatre in Liverpool doing pantomime and Duke Ellington was due shortly to appear there. It happened to be that he was going to use the same dressing-room that I was in. I left him a short note saying, "Please help yourself to drink," and so forth. He wrote me a lovely reply, being the kind man that he was, saying, "Hi there, thanks for the room, Eric ... " and so on, and signed it the Duke. And I lost the damn thing. *And* I didn't get around to going to his show, which is something I should have done ... '

Some of the Duke's courteous behaviour clearly rubbed off on Eric, for it was something I noticed shining through him down the years. He would always find a smile or a quip for anyone interested in him. The actor Tony Slattery recalled sharing a ride in a lift with him during which my father told Slattery that you can measure the character of a person by how they treat someone who is seemingly of no value to them. Maybe that's how he came to judge Duke Ellington so highly.

Eric always admired the past masters of comedy, accepted his peers of comedy, and distrusted the youth of comedy that was breaking through in the early Eighties. 'Contemporary comics concern me slightly,' he said. 'I worry because I feel there is very little talent coming up, but maybe I'm saying that because I am an old pro now. I don't know. Perhaps I envy the fact that the newcomers are young and they have it all to go ... '

That's very telling, because I know my father so enjoyed his life and, perhaps as a direct consequence, always seemed to see himself and Ernie as the new kids on the block, despite the passing years. The fact that it had taken some twenty years to make a decent career and reach many millions of people was perhaps the root cause of their appearing forever new, fresh, vibrant, and of the moment. And I find the strangest thing of all, which sort of confirms this theory, is that when I watch new DVDs compilations or repeats of their shows I discover there *is* a timeless immediacy about them. It is almost as though they have stepped out in front of the camera that week; not the forty-odd years ago that it really is. Much of that is due to their immense talent as performers – the voices of ageless comedy delivered through two middle-aged men bickering over mostly surreal issues. As comedian and writer Ben Elton once observed, they were 'the greatest alternative comedians of all time'. Much of it is in the writing of Eddie Braben – the affectedness of Ernie and the puncturing wit (Groucho and Phil Silvers-style) of Eric towards both Ernie and the numerous guest stars. It's the product of complete teamwork.

Sir Michael Parkinson – universally known as 'Parky' – told me, 'What made it interesting for me with Eric, was the fact that yes, we came roughly from the same part of the world – the north of England – but that Eric came from a long line of great names of northern comedy who were my heroes.

'I was very aware of the variety hall tradition: Sandy Powell, Norman Collier, Jewell and Warris, Jimmy Tarbuck, Les Dawson. I admired these comedians enormously as they and their predecessors were not so much part of my childhood as my birthright. When eventually I came to do the Parkinson shows, I wanted to meet as many of these heroes as I possibly could.

'I managed to interview Sandy Powell, for God's sake! I managed to persuade the producer to allow him to do his famous vent act – filmed for posterity. Without doing that type of thing it would have been lost for ever.

'And then at the height of their fame I interviewed Eric and Ernie for the first time,' he says with a wistful smile. 'You don't get stars like Morecambe and Wise now. It's hard for people today to understand just how truly big they were. I mean they were superstars. They were colossal. And television's changed, so we won't see the like of them again.'

I remember their first appearance in 1972 very clearly. It was the show when my father famously retold the story of the night of his heart attack in November 1968 when he and Ernie had been working near Leeds. It was also the show in which the previous guest before them was Raquel Welch.

'One of the smartest moves Raquel Welch ever made in her career was saying to me, "No, I'm not going to go on with them!"

'I'd been talking to Raquel in the interview about her equipment arriving, and as soon as Eric and Ernie came on after her piece, Eric said, "My equipment *never* arrived!"

'It was interesting to see how Eric and Ernie could do a spot like they did on my show, and manage to give each other individual space,' says 'Parky'. 'It would have been very easy for Eric to overwhelm Ernie, but Eric knew when to involve his partner, and Ernie knew when to sit back and let Eric go. That takes a very deep understanding, which presumably comes from years of treading the boards together.'

Healthy, Wealthy ...
and Wise

*'I first met up with Ernie Wise when we were thirteen-year-olds doing turns on **Youth Takes a Bow**. I remember what I thought of him then. The only word for it was "strange". But now I know him so much better I've changed that. He's "very strange".'*

The beginning of the 'golden era' for Morecambe and Wise was heralded by the words 'Thursday 25th December 1969 BBC1, 8.15pm–9.15pm, Guests: Susan Hampshire, Frankie Vaughan, Nina, Ann Hamilton and Janet Webb'. Those were the details in *Radio Times* of their first-ever Christmas special, a seminal event which would change everything.

With the nation's unified love and expectation of the wonderful *Morecambe and Wise Christmas Shows* came a fame they had dreamed about as kids but never fully believed would be theirs; and with it a wealth that likewise went way beyond the modest expectations of their youth. And that was all fine and dandy. So what were the drawbacks?

I think that from my father's point of view the stress of not only having spent years attaining what they set out in search of, but of now having endlessly to work to consolidate it, did some harm to his physical health. From having been hopefuls without much pressure beyond the basic desire to survive in the business – and they'd always managed that OK – they were catapulted into being the top act on the comedy heap. As frightening and heady as it was remarkable, this new situation placed great pressure on them. Many times before I've said that my father was never fully able to deal with responsibility and stress, and this he himself readily confirmed over the years.

My mother deliberately geared our home life to making everything easy for her husband, and we all understood, and for the most part did our best to meet, the need to make allowances for genius. But in the working environment, following Morecambe and Wise's sudden elevation from what Eric jokingly described as 'a cheap music-hall act', they were now in all seriousness dubbed 'the nation's favourites'.

From Ernie Wise's standpoint the downside of this success was that his role as straight man – one which even today has a vaguely derogatory connotation – was being given far closer critical scrutiny. This was right and understandable in so much as Eric was receiving the same examination for his comedic talents. But the fact remains that the lot of the straight man, which is a topic that surfaces repeatedly in this book, was and is a particularly tough one; and while Eric was arguably over-glorified for his unquestionable comic gifts, Ernie was ludicrously devalued for his own gifts. And gifts they clearly were, for what is a double act without two performers? As comedy double act Mitchell and Webb point out, Eric and Ernie are inseparable because what makes the comedy work is the combination of the two personalities.

Negativity has hovered over Ernie's career ever since those original media examinations and mud eventually sticks. So perhaps it is hardly surprising, if not very pleasant, that over the decades several people have said to me, 'We love your dad but hate Ernie.' I've always found this reaction slightly shocking. 'Love' and 'hate' are such strong, emotive words to use in this context. We're talking

Left to Right: The author, Gail, Melody (her horse!), Joan and Eric. This was taken in the Morecambes' paddock which fronts the house where Joan Morecambe still resides. The photo is a publicity still from one of many articles about Eric during the late sixties and early seventies. This one was taken circa 1969.

On board the QE2 ship April 1970. Eric gagging with his glasses – this time he has two straight-men! Glasses became such a huge part of Eric's persona. At this time he had only just begun fooling around with them and he looks slightly bemused by his own horseplay. The glory days of the glasses as a visual gag were still a few years away and he would use such opportunities as these to try out an idea or two.

about a wonderful comedy duo, not two dictators. It basically shows a lack of appreciation of the straight men of the comedy world. It says that we love funny men but don't understand why they need a partner. Comedian Paul Merton said, 'I believe the people who don't understand how these things work denigrated Ernie Wise down the years. It is the two of them together that is superb: there has never been a better double act. And Ernie is more than a straight man, but, if we have to use that term, there was never a better straight man.'

Dominic Cavendish picked up on this in a piece in the *Daily Telegraph* in 2007. Writing about Ernie's development under the influence of their BBC scriptwriter Eddie Braben, he said: 'Wise had always been short, dapper, reassuringly ordinary. Now, as brought home by the daft playlets that ended each episode, he had aspirations to be a playwright, giving Morecambe even more opportunities to bring him down to earth.' And he went on to quote an obser-

Left to right: Joan Morecambe, Eric, and family friend Margaret Day seated on the terrace of Eric and Joan's back garden overlooking the pond. Photo by the author circa mid-seventies.

Madge Shaw with Eric on his terrace. Madge was a neighbour of Eric's mother Sadie, and knew Eric from when he was a boy. This was the one and only visit to Eric's Harpenden house. The photo was taken by Madge's son.

vation my father made about his partner's transformation. 'What Eddie Braben did for Ernie,' Eric said, 'was to make him into a person. Before, anybody could have played his part. Not now. Ernie is his own man.'

The late, truly great Tony Hancock, referring to Clapham and Dwyer, a touring variety double act of the first half of the twentieth century, said of Billy Dwyer: 'He bore out what I have always felt about these comedy partnerships; that the straight man is invariably much funnier than he is credited with being.'

It's a commonplace to say that you can't have one without the other, but what some people fail to notice about double acts is the emotional support that the two partners give each other, and particularly in the early years, when the failures are far more frequent than the successes. Ernie kept Eric grounded and was responsible for making him great. Certainly Eric was a very funny man since the day he entered showbiz – according to some of the interviewees in this book,

Eric about to tee off with his golfing partner Arthur Askey looking on. Eric took to golf big time in the mid-sixties through friends and colleagues like Askey and Val Doonican. Later he joined his local golf course conveniently placed at the end of his garden. He played regularly until the mid-seventies, at that point deciding that not only the frustration of the game was doing him more harm than good, but the pettiness of the people he played against was spoiling what he saw as something that should be fun. It was then he turned more to fishing and bird-watching.

funny from the moment he was born – but without the stabilizing presence and unique abilities of Ernie at his side, he might have been a lost talent, a comic run adrift without the support he needed to be the comedian we came to love and even idolize. Ernie knew just when to pull Eric back and just when to let him go: Eric was the loose cannon, Ernie the grounded, calming influence.

'Ernie gave Eric something to bounce off,' commented Paul Merton. 'If Ernie slipped up, Eric would be in like a shot: and if all else failed, he could slap him around the face and say, "You can't see the join." Brilliant stuff!'

But the greatest reality check of all is to understand that Eric himself said he could never have done any of it without Ernie. Notice, he didn't say he could never have done it without a partner. For Eric it *had* to be Ernie. And in an interview nearly thirty years ago he said, 'There is no one better … he is the greatest

This must be a press photo of Eric and Joan – it's too well-constructed to be a happy snap! I know it is taken in Eric and Joan's living-room because the chair on the far left of the photo is the one which appears on the front cover, paperback version, of the author's book **Memories of Eric***. The chair has since made the lengthy journey right across to the other side of the room where it remains at the time of writing!*

straight man in the country.' Ernie was there to complement Eric. And he never sought to get one over him by trying to win the laughs himself or by complaining – publicly, at least, and that is where it mattered – that Eric was getting most of the plaudits. That must have taken a good deal of courage and common sense, because Ernie could be very, very funny when he was allowed to be, which by design was mostly when away from the cameras. And when you're in a double act it is imperative that you find your partner funny. As author John Fisher says, 'The real key to [Morecambe and Wise's] popularity is in the loyalty and camaraderie that binds the two, each obviously regarding the other as a genuinely funny man, a camaraderie never impaired in the audience's view by Ernie's show of pomposity or Eric's barbed defiance. The point is that for all Eric's protestations to the contrary – Morecambe and Wise – well, you really can't see the join.'

oops
shampoo

The Hedgehog

A selection of never-before-seen photographs from the album of family friend Amanda Davidson, née Kilburn.

'Eric and Ernie had done it the hard way,' points out Michael Parkinson, alluding to the oneness of their relationship. 'They came through the halls and basically served an apprenticeship which doesn't exist now. I'm sure being stars on television was never easy, but it must have been better than stepping out to unforgiving audiences at the Glasgow Empire to the sound of your own foot-falls! You have to be a very special type of person to survive and become stars like Morecambe and Wise did.

'But think of it; twenty-five years after your Dad died and ten years after Ernie died, and we can sit here together and still laugh just by reminiscing.'

Joan and Eric on the QE2 cruise April 1970. Eric wearing the author's 'John Lennon' hat.

I was watching the latest Morecambe and Wise DVD put together by the BBC. It's arguably the best of the lot in that it covers what is left of their first series in 1968, when Eric and Ernie were still in formulaic straight-man-funny-man mode and the scripts were, as ever, supplied by Sid Green and Dick Hills. In other words, it is the Morecambe and Wise of the ATV Lew Grade years but in their earliest BBC incarnation. While it's of historic inter-est to see the little that still remains from this first series, what makes the DVD somewhat remarkable, and this is an accidental by-prod-uct of the compilation, is the contrast between the two definitive eras of the first series in 1968 and the second series in 1969. And it would be the second series which would

Family Christmas. The author occupying his father's head-of-table chair for the two minutes it took for Eric to take this photo. Eric adored the festive season, and the fact he was relaxed enough to get into some Christmas Day photography shows his mind was not always on his own Christmas evening show.

Eric by his Harpenden swimming pool.

Eric in conversation with family friend June Rendall.

define how their double act would become loved and remembered, it seems, for ever.

The one reason for this is that by the time this second series had been screened, Eric had nearly died at the age of forty-two from his first heart attack. Hills and Green – perhaps in fear of his failing to recover from it – had abandoned ship for other projects, and now Eddie Braben was not only at the helm in terms of writing much of their material, but had redefined Eric and Ernie's working relationship to make it more akin to Laurel and Hardy in content and style, as discussed earlier. Essentially, Eddie had developed in script form the Eric and Ernie he discovered when meeting them – warm, gentle, caring, and closer than brothers. And this he had to do because, he was the first to admit, he didn't believe in the double act in its original format. 'No one can be that stupid!' he said, going on to add, 'What we never saw [in the ATV series] was the genuine warmth that existed between them. I always felt that Ernie was too hard; too abrasive. He had this charming innocence, but you never saw that in the act. He was the typical feed.'

A day or two after watching the DVD I came across a *Daily Telegraph* article about this very product which correctly noted that this second series was 'when "Bring Me Sunshine" becomes their signature tune'. But what I liked most about the piece was its summing-up: 'Watching this DVD is a reminder that, although they sometimes had duff lines, they never gave a duff performance. Though the age they embodied grew stale to the palate, they were fresh like no other double-act – before or since.' That nails it for me. It is what I have always said and always believed: Eric and Ernie transcended the fashions, attitudes, politics, and so on of any period in which they worked. It is as though they were grabbed from a timeless place and put in front of a camera and allowed to chat and occasionally run riot. Each show almost resembles an exceptionally well-made home movie: 'This is Eric and Ernie in a studio garden having fun' sort of thing. 'Here we see them dancing down the street like Gene Kelly.'

What each show *doesn't* do is deliberately and frequently reflect upon life as it was lived at that time. This is of paramount importance to their continued success for, like Laurel and Hardy, while they clearly come from a specific time-frame, what they are seen doing within that timeframe is timeless. Their material contains so few pointers to the nature of the era that they cannot become victims of changing outlooks and tastes.

Larking about on board the QE2.

Under Braben's influence both Eric and Ernie became distinct characters. Ernie more so, perhaps, through his on-screen pretensions to be a playwright, but Eric too was sharper than in previous decades. Eddie had seen to that, washing away the gormless funny man of yesteryear as if he had never existed.

Dominic Cavendish, again in the *Telegraph*, describes Eric as 'that manic-limbed, maverick-minded man-child, [who] could turn, say, some throwaway chatter about his hand ("My hand, if you realise, my hand has been everywhere with me") into a pitch-perfect comic soliloquy, punctuated as ever by nudges of those black-rimmed specs.'

Eric's Groucho-cum-Phil Silvers repartee with their guest stars is another key to their great success. Of their guest stars, Ernie once said, 'No one has ever been difficult to work with during rehearsal, or objected to the sketches

Eric, the non-swimmer, ironically seen in his pool for a magazine advert.

Eric eavesdropping at drinks' party. He could never resist a camera and had such masterly skill at using the lens to his best advantage. A truly rare talent. We have so many photos in our collection where Eric intercepts from the sidelines to make his presence felt!

Eric eavesdropping at drinks' party. He could never resist a camera and had such masterly skill at using the lens to his best advantage. A truly rare talent. We have so many photos in our collection where Eric intercepts from the sidelines to make his presence felt!

we've asked them to play in.' And Eric added, 'We're always amazed at how professional all our guests are. None of them is ever late for rehearsals. Well, all except one – Glenda Jackson. She went to our old rehearsal place … No one had told her we'd moved!'

Eric recalled *Dad's Army* star Arthur Lowe appearing on one of their shows (along with most of the *Dad's Army* cast, if I recall correctly): 'Arthur Lowe is another whose professionalism impressed us. You could give him fifteen pages of script and the next morning he would turn up word-perfect.'

Arguably their most famous guest star in their most famous show (which included Shirley Bassey and the 'boot' incident) was André Previn conducting Grieg's Piano Concerto with Eric as pianist. Eric said, 'André arrived on Monday morning for rehearsals and said he was sorry but would have to miss rehearsals the following day because he wanted to visit his sick mother. We nearly collapsed when he said she lived in Los Angeles … When we started rehearsals he was word-perfect. We thought he'd been learning his lines on the long flights. But he hadn't. He learned the script by torchlight in the back of a taxi coming from the airport!'

Michael Parkinson told me, 'The Morecambe and Wise Andre Previn sketch will last as long as human beings have a sense of humour. It's a genuinely classic piece of comedy.'

But, amid all the spectacle of guest stars and lavish sets, Morecambe and Wise worked so well on TV because of the relationship between two middle-aged men – a surreal relationship of remembered schooldays sleights, crushes on the opposite sex, and contretemps with teachers.

'Eric and Ernie transcended the fashions, attitudes, politics, and so on of any period in which they worked.'

Eric and Ernie's careers progressed steadily along their chosen path but there were two notable diversions. One was their journey into film-making, the other a few appearances on *The Ed Sullivan Show* in New York. Both occurred during the sixties, which in itself is illuminating as they pre-date two other colossal events in their lives – Eric's first and near-fatal heart attack and their move from ATV to the BBC, where their star rose meteorically. The heart attack meant a temporary (though it was to prove permanent, at least as a double act) break from making big-screen films, and their arrival at the BBC to make *The Morecambe and Wise Show* brought about the new comedy team of Morecambe and Wise … and Braben. And, with the great John Ammonds in charge of production, the team was complete.

Eddie Braben, a Liverpudlian scriptwriter who had written for many, including the likes of Ken Dodd, was, as already mentioned, the first member of any creative team involving Morecambe and Wise to transform their professional personas. The days of Eric as the classic gormless funny man of the variety halls, and Ernie as the classic aggressive, know-it-all straight man, were all at once over. There was to be no gentle drift into the new comedy format – Eric and Ernie's first outing under Braben at the BBC introduced them as the polished and complete article. Braben created in Ernie Wise a man of some affectation who believed he wrote better plays than wot Shakespeare did! Eric he changed little, said Braben himself: it was more about taking out the simpleton and general fallibilities of his implausible stage persona. Eric, with his love of Groucho Marx and Phil Silvers, was in any case already redefining his own screen persona, becoming a sharper, shrewder funny man. This meant a slight shift away from his heroes Laurel and Hardy – though not in the mechanics of how his and Ernie's act worked – and into a faster-paced, ad-libbed style of humour where everything was delivered with energy and there was less emphasis on the traditional double-act staple of the idiot and the bigger idiot. What we now had, thanks to Braben, was one character who was worldly and superior but naive and pretentious (Ernie) and another who was devious and easily capable of pulling the wool over his partner's eyes while simultaneously protecting him from outside forces (Eric). What made this relationship an improvement on the standard double act of the time – including Eric and Ernie's partnership on ATV – was that both Eric and Ernie were free to have genuine personas: no longer were they tied to the strict format of stooge and funny man, which had

Andre Previn with Eric and Ernie. The author's favourite M&W piece of work, and also Eric's personal favourite piece of their own work.

A few years after Andre Previn attempted to conduct Grieg's Piano Concerto with Eric as soloist, 'Mister Preview' makes a brave return to the M&W show.

Eric posing for the press in son Steven's Go-Kart.

been on display for over a century in music halls and then variety venues. Also this was the era in which Morecambe and Wise brought choreographer-producer Ernest Maxin into the mix to give their shows the Hollywood touch.

'No longer were they tied to the strict format of stooge and funny man, which had been on display for over a century in music halls and then variety venues.'

'If Ern had his way, and this is just my opinion,' wrote Eddie Braben in his memoir *The Book What I Wrote*, 'I think he would have been very happy if the shows had all been one long Hollywood-style musical with perhaps a couple of comedy routines in between.'

For his part Ernie Wise had always felt a hunger for Morecambe and Wise to be an established American act. And that might have happened.

New York!
New York!

'When I arrived I took a cab to my hotel, the Waldorf Astoria.
Although American hotels are very good, the room I'm in isn't!'

Half a decade before their hugely successful television collaboration with Braben, Eric and Ernie, at that time still in their original format, believed they were on the road to fame in America – about to metamorphose into a Hope and Crosby or Martin and Lewis. And this might well have happened despite Eric's lack of enthusiasm for the idea.

In a rather timely way, as I write this chapter my sister Gail has just received an email from a Morecambe and Wise fan in the United States, which, if it proves anything, shows that at least one person recalls their visits there.

Producer Ed Sullivan had seen their act at the London Palladium and, like the British audiences, took to them at once. An invitation to New York to appear on *The Ed Sullivan Show* followed and they accepted, as they did repeatedly over the next three or four years, the arrangement only ceasing for a while after Eric's heart attack in 1968. When he had recovered, the door was open once again, but by then he had had enough of many stressful things in his life. Sullivan, who greatly appreciated British comedians, before extending the honour to Eric and Ernie, had invited the talented Norman Wisdom on to his show.

Left to right: comedian Dickie Henderson, Danny la Rue, HRH Prince Philip, Eric. This will have been taken at a charity function. Moments later...

...We are amused!

In revisiting Eric's diaries, some parts of which have been published previously, I browsed through the section which covers the years they spent working in New York on *The Ed Sullivan Show*. They make great reading, if only because they give a colourful sense of time and place and small but incisive glimpses into Eric and Ernie's working relationship and where Eric's sensibilities lay, as well as his general state of health and mind. His references to air travel, hotels, and the general way of life paint a past, if not forgotten, era, as he delivers a glimpse of a more innocent, optimistic decade. These particular entries I include in full as that is how they were intended to be read. You can tell from some of the comments and observations and the general tone that the diary was written for a wider readership than just the author himself at a later date. The extracts record a time in Morecambe and Wise's career that has until now been vague, to say the least, but now at last we have some details of what went on during the visits to New York and how Eric came to feel about it all.

These entries, which my father recorded after Morecambe and Wise's arrival at the BBC, cover the final three appearances the double act made on a New York stage.

The first group of entries follow the order in which they appear in the diary, but they are entirely undated. Since the entries that come after these are headed 'November 1967', it is fair to assume that the previous trip was in the winter of 1966–7. References to the weather certainly suggest as much. Occasionally I have added comments between the entries to clarify or elaborate on what Eric is talking about.

35,000 feet up, so the pilot said. I'm not going to argue with him. At this moment I'm in a Boeing 707 1st Class, flying over the Atlantic to New York. Ernie and I are going to do a show for Ed Sullivan. This is now the tenth show we have done for Sullivan in America … Although I'm not keen on flying I must say I enjoy the trip. Mind you, I do get very good treatment. I'm met at Heathrow by Pan Am reps, and whisked off to a little VIP room. Also, I'm met at Kennedy by more Pan Am reps, and taken through very quickly. On Pan Am you are well looked after. You get a good meal, all you can drink and a film. You have to pay £1 extra for the film, but it helps to pass the seven hours.

When I arrived I took a cab to my hotel, the Waldorf Astoria. Although American hotels are very good, the room I'm in isn't!

I met Ernie at Ted Elkort's office at 4.30pm on 35 West 53rd. I stayed at the office until 7.30 so I could go out with Ted for a meal. But I was so tired I felt ill, so we just had a drink together, and I went back to the hotel. I was in bed at 9.30pm. It's just started snowing outside. It's very cold.

Waldorf – New York
Got up this morning 9.30am. Still snowing and very cold. It's 15 degrees below freezing!

I walked downstairs from the twenty-first floor, and took a walk around the block. Then I returned for breakfast. This afternoon, Ern and I went to the Sullivan office to have a word with Tim, the producer. He was quite happy with the bit we're planning to do.

It's late afternoon – 'Cocktail Hour' – which I'm all for! Had a couple of drinks at the Essex House, where Ernie is staying, then back to the hotel. Watched some TV, which if you compare to British TV ... well, to me they know nothing. Ate, then went to bed early.

While on this occasion the producer was happy with the piece Eric and Ernie had chosen to perform on the show, it was not always the case. In his autobiography Ernie talks of changes which had to be made to suit the sensibilities of the American public. I've always found this odd, considering it's the most violent 'civilized' country on the planet. 'Ed Sullivan was charm itself ... ' wrote Ernie. 'I would rate his performing skills rather lower than his entrepreneurial know-how ... Much of the material had to be adjusted to suit what we were told was the "Bible Belt" audience. The remotest reference, no matter how oblique, to anything which might just possibly be construed as "immoral" was cut ... We had a ventriloquist routine with a standard evening-suited dummy sitting on Eric's lap. I came up to him and said, "I never knew you were interested in it?"

'To which Eric replied, "I'm not any more. I'm too old. That's why I took *this* up!"

'Too risqué. The joke was cut ... Anyway, our act went through numerous changes but, in my opinion, if not Eric's, it still worked – just.'

Waldorf – New York, next day
Today is a hard day. Two or three run-throughs at the theatre on Broadway, now called 'The Ed Sullivan Theatre'. A quick lunch then a music run in the afternoon. Saw the names 'Morecambe and Wise' on the front of the theatre. First time on Broadway. Mind you, it won't be there for long – we do the show tomorrow, so it will by taken down by tomorrow night.

Got back to the hotel, and phone is flashing message. It's Fred Harris, an Englishman who lives in New York and works for the Grade-Delfont office. Also works for himself. Anyway, I said, 'Come round and have a drink, Fred,' which he did. We stayed drinking in the Waldorf as it was too cold to go out.

We slowly got pissed, then had a bowl of soup downstairs in the café. This would be 12.30. I then said 'Goodnight.' He didn't speak, managed to get into a cab and went home. I went to my furnace of a room and fell asleep instantly. Didn't even switch on the TV!

Next day
It's thick snow outside; it's thick hammers inside my head! It's 'show time' morning. Got to get down to the Sullivan Theatre for 9.15. Now try and be funny at that time in the morning! But it's got to be done.

We rehearse and hang about the theatre all day. Fred comes round before the show. Then the show is over. 'They' say it's gone well. I'm not happy about it, and nor is the 'Boy Wonder'*. But 'they' are, so much so Ed asked us out to

What the public never saw. The extreme rehearsals behind the Morecambe and Wise shows. This one shows them being guided through choreography for one of their many wonderful dance routines.

* Eric's nickname for Ernie.

dinner with him that night. We go to Danny's Hideaway on Lexington, and have a very informal and most enjoyable evening. Bed around 12.

Next day

Well, I'm going back home tonight. Back to 35,000 feet again, and this time I shan't be sorry. It's twenty-nine degrees below freezing, and that to me is cold! ... I've checked out of the hotel and taken all my cases to the Essex House. Taxi at 7.15, airport 8, VIP room 8.30. 9.15, not drunk but happy. Great. In the VIP room I met [the ballet dancer] Alicia Markova's sister. We had quite a long chat, both her and her sister are big fans, which never fails to amaze me. She's on the plane leaving before mine ...

The whole of the country [UK] was covered in a tremendous fall of snow ... ours was the first plane in that morning. Very thrilling. Really all this took place on Tuesday morning, but I'm writing on New York time!

It's a day off for the chauffeur as Eric takes the short cut to Tesco's!

Interesting to note in the above entries how Eric shows a snobbish tendency when mentioning, more than once, that he uses VIP lounges and travels first-class, yet great humbleness, to the point of dumbfoundedness, when showing genuine surprise at people telling him that they're big Morecambe and Wise fans. Note also that Eric and Ernie stayed in different hotels, whereas you'd think that for convenience they would stay in the same hotel but on different floors if it was a bit of privacy they were after. Once they were both married they stopped sharing a

Spot the famous faces! At the back are Brian Moore and 'Big' Ron Atkinson. To the far left is comedian Russ Abbot, with Jim Rosenthal sat to his right, while on the far right is Dickie Davies, sat next to Eric.

dressing-room, which is totally understandable, but while visiting another country I would have thought it pragmatic to be nearer each other. Maybe this was part of the technique which enabled them to stay working together for a total of forty-three years.

One thing my father couldn't disguise, and to be fair he didn't attempt to, was his delight at being out of America and back in England. This becomes more and more apparent as the entries continue. I should state that he was passionate about England and mildly suspicious of anything 'foreign'.

*The Queen,
delighted to be
meeting royalty!*

We jump forward a little, and he and Ernie are back in New York for *The Ed Sullivan Show*:

November 24 1967 New York

My God — it's weeks since I wrote anything in this book. I've had all the time in the world in which to do it, as since I finished Yarmouth I've done absolutely nothing. One record and two interviews for BBC radio. The TV shows that we did for the States are now coming out every three weeks in Britain*. The first one got to number one in the ratings. The second one came in at number 5 and the third one came in at number one again. It will be interesting to work out the average when the series is over.

It's nine-o-clock Friday morning the day after Thanksgiving. I'm having my continental 'jet' breakfast in my room at the New York Hilton — which is not a hotel I would stay at again. I prefer the Americana — or the others I've stayed in. Ern and self are over here to do a Sullivan show this Sunday. I'm watching TV at the moment, and it's 9.15 in the morning!

* Eric and Ernie did a run of shows geared to American audiences as a trial to see how their humour would go on that side of the Atlantic. Except for sales of some material from their BBC shows made many years later, it seems that despite a positive response they did no more TV shows specifically for the American market.

November 27

Ernie's Birthday!

I haven't as yet bought him anything but will. Probably something small, like a small TV set (Joke). Did the show last night. OK, but really it's like hitting your head against a brick wall. This can't do us much good. But the money is good: $9000 with tips! (Joke).

November 28

Today we saw Billy Marsh* who came over to see us and Norman Wisdom. He told me Jock Cochrane, an old friend of mine, died in England last week. Early in our career he did a lot for us. This afternoon we (Billy, me and Ern) went to the Sullivan office to have a talk with Bob Precht who is Ed's booking manager. He was happy with the show we did and would like us to do as many more as we want. So it looks like we will be back again in the New Year. He also mentioned a Broadway show,** but this is in the very early talking stage as yet. Billy is by devious ways trying to get us to do as much over here as possible, but I think it is only to make gains for his own ends.

* Billy Marsh was agent to Morecambe and Wise and this author's former employer. He instigated Eric and Ernie's first successful television series, which was for Lew Grade's ATV in 1961.

** Nothing came of the Broadway show idea, though ironically Morecambe and Wise would end up on Broadway, albeit by proxy, when in 2003 the West End play about their lives, *The Play What I Wrote*, transferred to the Lyceum on Broadway.

What I find fascinating about the almost everyday comments Eric penned above is that there is this clear distrust of their potential popularity in the States. He doesn't like the hotel; despite success he feels they are hitting their heads against a brick wall, and his agent Billy Marsh is apparently being devious in attempting to get them continued, well-paid work over there. Knowing Ernie as I did, I imagine his take on this time was altogether very different. Whenever Eric wanted something to happen in their career it tended to hap-

Joan and Eric with Liberace among others. They met up with Liberace several times both in the UK and America. Eric's mother-in-law Alice Bartlett was a huge fan of Liberace, so I imagine Eric contrived several meetings for her down the years.

pen. Did his heart attack exactly one year after these diary entries were written really mean they were destined never to make it big in America, or was it the perfect, unquestionable excuse not to have to pursue it any more? Certainly there were further interviews down the years – including one for Michael Parkinson's show – where Eric tended to throw water on the idea. His most memorable line, which I paraphrase, was, 'I won't say sidewalk for pavement or elevator for lift.' And he was quick to point out that it had taken them twenty years to become stars in Britain, so why go through all that again? Which is a fair point, though you could often see Ernie Wise wincing behind a tight-lipped grin and nod of agreement. This is where Eric and Ernie were at their best – they *did* always present a united front, even if it sometimes hurt. Ernie must have sensed, even at the time they were working in the States, that Eric was never going to give his all to making things happen out there, and that at best any success should be viewed as a by-product of their success in Britain. I wouldn't go as far as saying Eric was xenophobic, but there was more than a hint of his only being content when back in the UK, even it was after a fortnight's holiday anywhere abroad.

Ernie wrote in *Still On My Way To Hollywood* that Eric was concerned about doing shows in New York because 'it was an audience of millions of *Americans* who took a bit of time to warm to an English act'. The italics are his, so it is clear where the emphasis lies. Indeed he goes on to say, 'It was possibly the only time I became impatient with Eric.'

A further diary entry by Eric – short and solitary on its own page – reveals his realization that the only problem with America might be him. It comes just before what would be their last-ever trip over there to appear on Sullivan's show:

> *December 31 1967 Harpenden*
> *… Next week off to New York again. I'm not looking forward to it. But I never*
> *do. Sometimes I think there must be something wrong with me.*

And then he has arrived:

January 7 1968 Waldorf Astoria New York
It's thick snow outside. This trip the weather has really been cold. 15 below. I
hope the plane will take off tomorrow. It could have cleared by then. Ern and
I do the Sullivan again tonight. We will do the Marvo and Dolores bit. All the
crew think it's very funny. But I have been wrong before.

There's still a negativity seeping into his tone, as Eric never was wrong about what worked for Morecambe and Wise, so that he should imply he *might* be wrong is representative of the apathy these New York trips were invoking. It's even more interesting when put into the context of his health. No one, including Eric, knew that he had ten months of this annual ritual before his massive, near-fatal heart attack that coming November.

In further entries we see a continued strategy developing to keep Eric interested in making it big in the States, matched by his continued apathy towards the notion:

New York January 1968
We went to the Sullivan office today to meet the girl who is doing the 'Wall'*
bit with us. She's called Michelle Lee and was one of the leads on Broadway
and this film How To Succeed. *She is very pretty and also is keen to do it.*
(The Wall bit, I mean!) Bob Precht, Sullivan's director, asked us if we would
stay over until the weekend to do another show on Saturday. It's a tribute to
Irving Berlin's 80th birthday. So we said we would. It's also with Bing Crosby
and Bob Hope.

* A musical number in which Eric and Ernie flank the female sitting on a wall and both try to woo her in song. This develops into a bit of competition between the two of them and they start pulling each other over the wall, but they return to carry on singing. It degenerates into a total romp which culminates in the girl being pulled off the wall. This routine made its TV screen appearance in the sixties, with Millicent Martin playing the wooed female, and was re-enacted intact by The Right Size in David Pugh and Kenneth Branagh's 2001 West End tribute play *The Play What I Wrote*.

My father would have been particularly keen to meet Hope and Crosby, who had been such a successful big-screen double act over the previous two decades.

This reveals the incongruity of his dislike for everything that side of the pond alongside his great love, respect, and curiosity for the star names America had produced (even if Hope hailed from Lewisham, in London).

The undated entries of that week continue with Eric becoming more and more unable to be part of the New York world:

> *I was taken out to the Playboy Club by Fred* [Harris]. *We went to see a young comic. Fred thought he was good. I didn't rate him. Although it was a free night, the food was terrible.*

The next day:

> *Rehearsed all day with Michelle. Went to bed early without Michelle!!*

A rare photo of Eric not posing – on his patio in Portugal where he liked to work on M&W scripts despite supposedly being on holiday! Being a non-swimmer made working less of a burden to him; indeed, he really enjoyed it, inspired by the climate and the scenery.

The next day:

The day of the show. 9.15 at the theatre, saw our name outside. Must say it gives one a kick to see your name up on Broadway. At 9.30 we had a music call, then did what the Americans call 'Blocking', which is a camera run-through. Back at 12 in the afternoon for make up. At 1, a complete dress run, with the people out front. It went very well. They had no notes for us. Next show would be showtime at 8.

The show went great for us. It really did well.

The next day:

I didn't do much today. I got up late and had lunch at a Chinese restaurant. People knew me from the show the night before. I felt like walking about saying, 'Yes, I was on last night. Glad you liked it!' However, one can't do that. Although I know one or two that almost do that.

I stayed in most of the afternoon. Fred [Harris] *rang up at about 5pm and came over to the hotel at about 6.30pm. He had nothing lined up, so rang the George Abbott theatre to see if we could walk over and get tickets for* Darling of the Day. *It was very easy, so we went. The theatre was half full. (A pessimist would say half empty!) ... The show was lacking somewhere. Mind you, that is always easy to say. I know I couldn't have put it right. After the show, Fred and I went for a bowl of soup at some Broadway café. Home after, and a few drinks and kip.*

I find it interesting how in these entries my father apparently becomes aware of his own negativity as demonstrated in that marginally defensive line 'A pessimist would say half empty!' One of his greatest strengths, in my opinion, was that he was always so positive. Certainly he could get spiky at times, and was by no means someone you would have described as tolerant and patient, but he saw the world, for the most part, through sunny spectacles.

The next day:

This morning I had to meet Pat Kilburn*, in Saks on Fifth Ave. Or, as the Americans say, Fitavenooo. Pat came at 11 as arranged. She wanted to shop and buy some shoes and matching handbag. Which we did. I noticed while waiting for her in the shoe department that the American women treat the sellers like dirt. To me they do have a class distinction. But it's all of their own … The more I'm over here, the more I am glad I'm English – even British.

Pat and I went to the top of the Pan Am building for a quiet drink, which in New York is impossible. Then we caught a cab out to the airport to meet her husband, Mike, who was doing some biz there. Then we drove to their home in Wilmington, Delaware.

*An old friend from Harpenden, Hertfordshire, where Eric lived from the sixties until his death.

The next day:

Wilmington Delaware.

Mike isn't too well. Probably run down with the strain of the move over here. Pat, Erika and Amanda* seem fine, and the kids are well now, going to school and becoming very quickly a part of the scene out here ...

Pat drove me around the Dupont country ... I should imagine in Spring and Summer it must be very lovely. I only stayed the one night. I caught a train back to New York. Never having been on an American train I found it most interesting. They seem to run much more quietly than ours. The porter, just before we got into New York, made a speech: 'Ladies and Gentlemen, in a few moments we will be in Pennsylvania station New York. Please could I have your tickets and complaints. I'll take the tickets first.' Then he took our tickets and left, never to be seen again!

* Amanda Davidson née Kilburn, daughter of Mike and Pat, provided some of the unique previously unpublished photos in this book.

The next day:

New York.

Just rehearsed today. Spent a lazy day and bought a hat,* one of the Russian types, which is very popular out here, but will get laughs at home. But it's so cold here that it's necessary.

*When Eric returned to England, he continued to wear the hat all winter, calling it his 'Doctor Zhivago' look. And yes, we all laughed every time he wore it, which didn't deter him at all, of course, because getting laughs was what always motivated him.

The next day:

New York.

Had a band call this morning and rehearsed. Hung about the theatre till

Fred came with his nephew. Spent the afternoon with them in a bar on Broadway. Told stories about Jack Hylton.* At 5 we came back to the theatre to get ready for the show. This show is the Ed Sullivan tribute to mark Irving Berlin's 80th.

Bing Crosby went on first and kept going wrong. They had to do his bit three times. Even then he sang White Christmas *wrong. But they let it go. We followed Bing Crosby and did our Fred Astaire skit. It was one of the best things we have done out here. Bob Hope followed us and started to do jokes about heart transplants. Not really in good taste. Also had idiot boards all over the front rows.*

* The same Jack Hylton who started and guided Ernie Wise's career in his youth, and gave Eric his first break.

Another day off for Eric's chauffeur!

The next day:

Flew back to England with David Frost who fell asleep as soon as he sat down and I woke him up about five minutes before landing. He was coming home for three hours then flying back to New York!

And so, unbeknown to Morecambe and Wise at this time, ended their American extravaganza. Not that the drama stopped on Eric's return. His final entry in the New York section of his diaries reads:

Brian* met me in and took me home. I was sat down watching TV in the after-noon . . . when at 4.15 Gary runs in to tell me Gail had fallen off her horse and the horse had kicked her in the face knocking out her two front teeth. She looked a terrible mess. Joan got the doctor round and Mike (Doc) got Gail's dentist and had an X-ray done. She had one tooth splintered and the other one has been pushed up under her nose, and her top jaw had been fractured . . . She couldn't talk and looked one hell of a mess. However, it was arranged for her to go to hospital as soon as the swelling went down, which when you looked at her you thought it never would. What a black Sunday it's been.

* Eric's occasional driver before he employed Mike Fountain full-time .

Makin' Movies
(Part One)

'Arrived back from Portugal, and our villa over there is in a worse state than the house over here. Somehow you can't win. The weather was very nice – in the eighties. Over there we met some nice people – the Baron and Baroness Osterman [sic] of Germany. And a man called Christopher Wren, who is a direct descendant of the Christopher Wren. All were charming and live in the Algarve. But I feel that most of the other residents are mostly failures out there. They only seem to be scratching a living. They are the ones who say, 'Isn't the weather wonderful – you can't get this at home!' You won't get me going back. Not unless they are deported, and I feel some of them will be. No! At the moment I'm one of those unfashionable people who happen to love England. It's great to be back – weather and all!'

Eric photographed in the garden of his villa in Portugal by the author circa 1970.

The above diary entry for 15 October 1967, made by Eric one month before he and Ernie went to New York, emphasizes my father's

Outside the front door of the Morecambe villa, mid-seventies. Left to right: Eric's daughter Gail, family friend, Margaret Day, Eric, and Eric's mother-in-law Alice Bartlett. Photo taken by Joan Morecambe. Gail is clearly recovering from some leg surgery judging by the crutches. Remarkably Eric hasn't taken the opportunity of using them as a prop for this photo. He rarely missed such an opportunity when there was a camera in the vicinity!

Eric in his villa swimming pool in Portugal with son Steven. Photo by the author mid-seventies. Eric never learned to swim, which explains why he's clutching the side like his life depends on it!

distrust of anything remotely foreign. He was without doubt someone who never allowed himself to be particularly influenced by the weather, although naturally he didn't rejoice in constant winter rain and cold; but he never really complained about it because he felt very safe and secure in his home country. England is the country that made him – he made a marked distinction between England and Britain (as we saw in an earlier diary entry) – and he never would forget that, and consequently did not fully feel at ease when away from it. It contrasts with his more cosmopolitan lifestyle, so removed from his northern upbringing, this belief that the UK was the only place in which he could feel secure. How ironic he would find it to know that in my lumbering middle age I try to spend several months of each winter in the Algarve to escape the British winters, and much of this book was penned while there. That's just the sort of quirky little thing that would tickle him.

The diary entry dates from about a year and a half after my parents bought the land on which their villa was built. It never was supposed to happen. It certainly wasn't planned. We were on holiday there – the family's first visit to the Algarve – when some friends, Cyril and Muriel Coke, who owned a property virtually opposite this piece of land, encouraged my parents to buy. The location was beautiful, the weather perfect (as even my father agreed), so it is easy to understand why, within the two-week stay, papers were drawn up and they found themselves on the verge of owning a small piece of picturesque Portugal. A recent conversation with my mother reveals that is was Eric's spontaneity that made an idea a reality.

My brother, Steven, who was not born until five years after my parents built their villa, grew up, like me, with fond childhood memories of long summer holidays in the Algarve sunshine. Fast forward to winter 2006 and the two of us are making a nostalgic trip to see what the villa looks like now.

We were staggered. My father had always warned us that it was destined to 'do a Spain', as he put it. Not only had the coastline been submerged beneath a wave of whitewashed houses, hotels, and other developments, but the villa – our little piece of Portuguese paradise – was now lost in a large town that had appeared like some ghastly mirage across the landscape of this former tranquil farming commune. Pubs, clubs, restaurants, guesthouses, hotels, neon lights constantly flashing day and night, traffic pouring down streets that once had been our open pastures and a haven for all kinds of wildlife. Different wildlife now! This is what had happened to paradise. It was a considerable shock.

After Eric died my mother had kept the villa until the end of the eighties and nothing had really changed. Following an eighteen-year absence I discovered that a villa that had stood in the open countryside with distant views of the sea from its rooftop was now just one house in a town that hadn't before existed. The back garden, which once had allowed hundreds of grapevines to flourish at its far end, was now supporting an apartment block, with another one quickly going up near by. My father got it right: it had done a Spain.

'Eric and Ernie were still metamorphosing when they made their films.'

In between the holidays in Portugal that punctuated my father's working trips to New York, something else also developed that was perhaps just as inevitable as Eric and Ernie's wish to test their humour in America on Americans. They were serenaded into making movies. Not that they needed much serenading. Ever since my father had gone to the cinema as a kid and been dazzled by Cary Grant, Fred Astaire, Laurel and Hardy et al., and Ernie had been considered the British equivalent of Mickey Rooney, the glamour and glitz of the big screen had appealed greatly to them. Even today comedians who have a good TV shelf life soon enough end up in movies – Cannon and Ball, Ant and Dec, Lee Evans, Ricky Gervais, Mitchell and Webb – and, in the past, Eric and

above **First ever trip to the Algarve, April 1966. Left to right: Joan, Gary, Eric, Gail.** *I still return to the Algarve every winter for a few weeks to escape the grey lid of the UK. It's always a hugely nostalgic journey for me – so many memories and so few people with whom they were shared still remaining. Such is life!*

Ernie's peers Tony Hancock, Norman Wisdom and others also went the cinematic route to a greater or lesser degree. Tragically, most of them fail. It doesn't seem to stop them all from trying, which is to be congratulated even if those on the outside can't help but feel they are allowing the doubts to be suppressed by the sheer challenge.

For Morecambe and Wise, still Lew Grade's top comedy stars at ATV, it was sooner rather than later that it happened. With that wonderful thing called hindsight, I can't help thinking that the whole three-movie affair for Rank at Pinewood Studios would have been just that bit better – more polished and more complete – had Eric and Ernie ended up on the cinema screen *after* the changes brought about by scriptwriter Eddie Braben and described in the previous chapter. That is the problem I have: Eric and Ernie were still metamorphosing when they made their films. Fundamentally they were captured by the big screen five years too soon. Accepted that the films work on various levels –

especially zest, innocence, location – and the boys were still very funny together; that hadn't changed since childhood. But they weren't the finished article they could have been. And when the chance eventually came around again, both men were too old to present themselves as they had been at their BBC peak. Their film *Night Train to Murder* did not receive cinematic release and would disappear virtually unnoticed except by their true fans. Eric himself died shortly before it was first shown publicly, on television, in 1984.

The fact that, back in the early and mid-sixties, Eric and Ernie had missed out on becoming the Morecambe and Wise of their peak years wasn't anyone's fault. They weren't to realize they would leave Lew Grade in 1967 and move to the BBC, where a new scriptwriter they'd never before met would be instrumental in reinventing and redefining them. Or that a massive heart attack at the age of just forty-two would make the idea of doing any further big-screen outings a matter of little or no interest to Eric. Sometimes I'd ask him if he intended to make another movie, but he was evasive and uncertain. 'Might get round to it,' he would say, but you could tell that he was a man safe in his own environment – the TV studio – so why take any chances? Also, he felt they never were given any really decent film scripts, and by way of example he cited the *Pink Panther* scripts which had been so successful for Peter Sellers. So in a way it is a kind of blessing that Eric and Ernie made it to the big screen at all: that they had their opportunity to do *something*, however limited.

'As a very spontaneous act they were dependent on audience reaction.'

It should be noted that these were not bad films. Admittedly they do little justice to Eric and Ernie, but that is because the Eric and Ernie they became – the ones we grew to know and love through their fantastic Christmas shows – had still to be created. The Eric and Ernie of the films were still more akin to the acts of the music-hall era like Abbot and Costello. Their transformation into the

new Laurel and Hardy had not happened, yet nowadays the films do tend to be judged on who they became rather than who they were when they made them, which is slightly unfortunate.

Furthermore, Eric and Ernie's humour was not the type to transfer to the movies. They were not comic actors in the mould of the brilliant Peter Sellers or Ronnie Barker or David Jason. As a very spontaneous act they were dependent on audience reaction. They were never as visually frantic or character-based as the Marx Brothers: qualities which might have allowed them to be really brilliant without the intimacy of the audience and the studio that their brand of humour and technique demanded.

Actor Fulton Mackay and Eric in a still from Eric and Ernie's somewhat lacklustre last outing together, the 1984 film Night Train to Murder.

p. 152–153
Stills from Eric and Ernie's third and final cinematic outing for the Rank Organization, The Magnificent Two.

They kicked off with *The Intelligence Men* (1964) and rounded it all off with *The Magnificent Two* (1967). And in between was a little gem of a film, which has a big following to this day, called *That Riviera Touch* (1966).

All three films were produced by Hugh Stewart and the first outing, *The Intelligence Men*, was directed by Robert Asher. One of the film's guest stars was Francis Matthews, who not only worked with Eric and Ernie several times over many years but maintained a friendship with them both over many decades.

I caught up with Francis at his home in Surrey before he was leaving for yet another performance in the West End play *Cabaret*. I'd always been eager to meet him, for he had been a childhood hero of mine from nearly forty years

earlier when he starred in BBC's first drama series in colour, *Paul Temple*. He had fond memories of both the Morecambe and Wise double act and the times they spent and worked together.

'I was a bachelor actor in the fifties and sixties, living in West Hampstead,' he told me. 'I was invited to some party in Bayswater – there were always parties going on back then – and I didn't really know anyone there. But Eric and Ernie were there. They arrived late because they were on a show at the Palladium, I think. I'd seen them in panto when I was even younger. So as soon as I saw them at this party I had something to talk to them about. We got along really well, but the next time I saw them was a few years later when I took the offered role in *The Intelligence Men*.'

Francis remembered the film vividly because it gave him the opportunity to work alongside not just Eric and Ernie but also his two closest friends in show business, Terrance Alexander and Bill Franklin. 'This was like an accolade. I was gobsmacked with joy,' he recalls. 'When we started working with Eric and Ernie at Pinewood, Robert Asher, the director, and the film's producer, Hugh Stewart, who was also producer of the Norman Wisdom vehicles, were always

keen to under-crank all the time, which basically makes people on film look like they're moving quicker than normal speed. Eric would say to Robert, "Please don't do that. It's not very funny. It's all right for Norman, but not for us." I thought that was a particularly perceptive observation.'

The thing that struck me as Francis reminisced is how friendly the set clearly was. 'We were all friends from the beginning,' he said. 'Bill, Terry, Me, Eric and

Ernie all gelled. I suppose it was because we were having such fun. Eric was a huge generator of good energy. Every one had to have a good time.'

Francis recalled talking to Eric about the late Bill Franklin, who will for ever be remembered by those old enough as the man who suavely delivered his lines in the Schweppes ad on television, spreading the catchphrase 'Shh, you know who!' 'Eric told me that he found Bill really funny,' said Francis. 'And Bill was a funny man, by the way: a great sense of humour. But it was very black humour and often quite cruel and dismissive. And Eric continued by saying, "Bill does-n't really do Funnies, he does Hurties!" That expression has always stayed with me. Wonderful! But they got along really well – they loved each other. It must be the thing of opposites attracting.'

Then Francis told me about rehearsing the film's debriefing scene, where Eric did a routine that became famous through their ATV shows in the sixties: he puts his hand under the other person's chin (mostly Ernie's) and says, 'Get out of that – yer can't, can yer?'

'I was the MI5 man, called Grant, I think,' explained Francis. 'I had a brief-case on a desk, and Eric, as a spy, came in for debriefing and started saying things like, "I want that thing … the thing with the gun; and the shoe thing … "Then he started doing the can't-get-out-of-that bit, saying, "Now if you were holding that briefcase … I'll show you. Can I borrow your briefcase, Mr … er … ?" And I at once say, "Do, do," and go to fetch the briefcase. And Eric ad-libbed, "Thank you, Mr Do-Do!" This stuck, of course, and Robert kept it in for the final take. And Eric took it a stage further. If you watch the film, every scene I'm in after that scene, he calls me Mr Do-Do. There's one line he ad-libbed where Eric has to go somewhere and he says, "Can Mr Do-Do come?" He was instinctively funny.'

Lunch on the first day of filming was another event Francis recalled. 'Eric made me smile because he said to me, "Are you going for lunch?" "Yes!" I told him. "Can I come?" What a question! The co-star of the film asking if he can come for lunch with me! So off we went to the main dining room for lunch, and as we go in Eric says, "Where are the stars? Show me all the big stars. Point them out, Fran." He was the kid in the sweet shop. But of course Eric expected to find the room crammed with the likes of Cary Grant, but other than Richard Harris there was nobody. I turned to Eric, who looked a bit despondent, and said the truth, "You and Ernie are the biggest stars in this room." Eric wouldn't have it, though. "No, no, no … I mean the film stars." "But Eric," I said, "You *are* a film star. You're here making a film, and you're the one every one else wants to meet.'"

Francis had been telling Eric a lot about his wife, Angela. 'By a happy coincidence she was at the same time filming an American TV series at the studios with Peter Graves called *Court Martial*. I'd pop over to her set every now and then, and on one occasion she was able to join us all for lunch. When she arrived for lunch, Eric walked straight up to her and said, "Oh, hello, love!" Then to me, "Is this the Elizabeth you keep talking about? Oh no, it's your wife – I'm sorry." And of course when he went to shake her hand as he said all this, he did the thing of pulling his hand back and prodding the centre of his glasses. Do you know, he did that every time we met up!'

"Can I borrow your briefcase, Mr … er?" "Do, do." "Thank you, Mr Do-Do!"

While it was clearly a lot of fun on set, Francis was quick to point out that, for Eric and Ernie, making those three films for Rank was a huge change from doing TV and so there was a serious side to entering upon this new venture. I know myself how keen they both were at this time to become film stars – Ernie perhaps more than Eric, in that Ernie, just as he longed to make it big in the States, would chase the dream till his last breath – so to underachieve in this medium would have been a severe body-blow to them.

The middle picture, *That Riviera Touch*, was filmed in the late summer of 1965 on the Grande Corniche, a spectacular road which runs from Nice to Menton on the border with Italy. In his diaries Kenneth Williams wrote: 'There were

some very original things in this film, which was very well done. These two came out of it very well indeed – very much "innocents abroad" and at times a real note of pathos was established.'

Actress Suzanne Lloyd guest-starred in the film. 'I didn't have to audition for *That Riviera Touch,* amazing as that is,' she said. 'There was a body of my work for anyone to see. The producer, Hugh Stewart, met with me at Pinewood, and that was that.'

Suzanne recalled the first time she met up with Eric and Ernie. 'We met as we were getting on the plane, and we were all a bit nervous with one another, which is usual before a film. I'm sure they didn't know my work and were wondering who I was and who they were stuck with. We worked in different genres. I was aware of Eric and Ernie, but hadn't seen them on TV. I was told they were as funny as [Dean] Martin and [Jerry] Lewis and indeed they were.'

She was able to confirm that film-making was 'not the boys' level of com-

Eric on the balcony of the Sol-e-Mar hotel in Albufeira, Portugal. 1966. The balcony is still there – indeed the hotel has changed little in over forty years despite a major fire destroying scores of rooms.

fort', as she put it. 'They were improv specialists. They did it once on TV and that was that. In film they had to do it over and over, and matching was a nightmare for both of them.' Apparently this led to their becoming concerned that the spontaneity would not be there and that they wouldn't be able to keep the takes fresh, which of course is not a problem in television, where their shows were virtually shot live. I remember many studio visits in the seventies, and if there was a technical problem requiring a retake of a part of a scene, both Eric and Ernie would deliberately wrong-foot the audience on the retake by adding a gag or changing their dialogue, just so as to keep it fresh. Sometimes Eric would say to the studio audience, only half-jokingly, 'Clear your mind and pretend you didn't see that last bit.' On a film set, without an audience, you can change it as much as you like, but there is no one to judge what went before: you just hammer on, retake after retake, until it all matches.

'They did not give me any advice as to how to make a scene funny,' said Suzanne. 'I wish they had. But they were concerned about stepping on the director's toes, I think. They did ask me about "matching" from scene to scene and from time to time we spoke about it. I would have loved it if they had taken me aside and given me some pointers.'

A particular point Suzanne Lloyd made, and one which informed how different my father was when working in this new medium, was his seriousness in making the film deliver its very best. 'Eric was not always "on",' she explained. 'This was hard for them. I cannot stress this enough. They had a lot riding on this film and they knew they were not in their element. But that doesn't mean there weren't laughs. There were a lot. The crew had a devil of a time not ruining a take by laughing out loud. And the Khartoum crew and cast would come over to be entertained. They had to stop that because the set was getting too noisy, and besides, they were drinking all our tea and eating our biscuits!'

My personal favourite scene from the film is the balcony scene when Eric is trying to seduce Suzanne's character, Claudette, with a song, and he's miming to Ernie's vocal. I was pleased that Suzanne too thought it the best scene.

'The boys had a good time with that one. Also in the dining room with Ernie trying to eat frog legs and snails without throwing up. That scene didn't require acting.'

'The crew had a devil of a time not ruining a take by laughing out loud.'

My mother tells me that the late summer of 1966 in the South of France is one of the happiest memories she has of her years with Eric. Suzanne Lloyd recalled of the times away from the cameras, 'Their wives were in the South of France and I remember liking them both, but then my husband knew Tony Curtis and we hung out with Tony and his wife and daughter. I can't remember socializing much with the boys.' But there was much socializing going on. Warren Mitchell and Lionel Jeffries were out there filming, and with or without Suzanne, the boys met up with Tony Curtis. There is a photo commemorating the occasion.

Suzanne's final comment is so consistent with the views of everyone I've talked with while working on this book. 'I liked the boys very much. Eric was thoughtful and considerate. Ernie was always smiling. They did not have a mean bone in their bodies. I was saddened to hear when they passed on. Too soon for both.'

Eric and Ernie's final big-screen outing, *The Magnificent Two*, was a strange film. Considering it was supposed to be a comedy, it was rather violent in places and drew critical fire for this reason. But for me this is one of the film's few strengths: it pulls away the safety net and makes what is a lightweight and irritatingly preposterous story suddenly a bit more engaging, a bit edgy. It led to talk of further films, but Eric said he didn't want to make any more if it involved Robert Asher or Cliff Owen as he felt they were too concerned with their own decisions and therefore less receptive to external suggestions. He also felt they had personal distractions on set, which he found disconcerting as it detracted from the 100 per cent commitment required to make a bunch of half-decent films.

The basic storyline is that two salesmen, played by Eric and Ernie, travel to South America to sell their products and become entangled in a revolution. It's the story of Eric having a doppelgänger and having to replace him after this lookalike (well, he wears the same hat and glasses) is bumped off. Eric has to take on his identity and later becomes ruler of the South American country when the revolution is at an end. Far-fetched in the extreme – Hans Christian Andersen would have blanched at the script – the film still contains Morecambe and Wise's irrepressible enthusiasm and joie de vivre. Also, no one plays it for laughs – except for Eric and Ernie, and even they keep it within the characters they are portraying – which makes it more acceptable as a film than it might otherwise have been.

On making the first of their three movies Eric had commented, 'We want to bring to the films the same originality we've brought to television. We don't want them to be just typical British comedies with all the usual ingredients.' Sadly, Eric's must have been a lone voice. The originality they brought to television comedy went adrift on the big screen, although to give all three films credit where it's due, they were not typical British comedies with all the usual ingredients. They were just too odd for that accusation to ever stick.

I'm not convinced that employing their TV scriptwriters, Dick Hills and Sid Green, to be their film scriptwriters was the best of moves. I can understand the security they felt in doing this — the continuity of working with the team that had helped to make them big stars on TV. But they needed big-screen writers — writers used to a medium that was new to the four of them.

Eric and Ernie's film era came and went, but countless are the times I've been watching some obscure cable channel and up comes one of them, transporting me back to blurry yet happy days.

Makin' Movies
(Part Two)

'Yes, I'll always remember the first big laugh I got professionally. I can also remember the last big laugh I got. It was the same one.'

It comes as a big surprise to many people – including me when I set out on the journey that ended up as this book – that in the last three or four years of his life Eric Morecambe did three theatrical-release film projects that in no way involved Ernie Wise. I probably knew at the time, but with the passing years had forgotten. It was certainly a thrill to be reintroduced to them.

The first two of these films were based on Sir John Betjeman's poetry and called *Betjeman's Britain* (1980) and *Late Flowering Love* (1981). They were narrated by Betjeman himself, which was a particularly satisfying element of the project. The third film, *The Passionate Pilgrim* (1984), like the other two, was directed by Charles Wallace.

In London I caught up with Charles, the brains behind the films,

A publicity-rigged shot by Eric's swimming pool. To add a sense of activity a few 'extras' were called in, including Eric's chauffeur Michael Fountain, who ironically now lives in Morecambe and who still is in contact with the Morecambe family.

to find out more about this trio of screen releases starring my father as a solo actor of which hitherto little was known. 'I had this idea of dramatizing some of Betjeman's poems,' explained Charles. 'They'd already been set to music, and I thought I'd just take it a stage further. There was one poem called "Indoor Games Near Newbury", which is basically a tale of a children's Christmas party. In the verses there was talk of a "funny uncle". Initially I'd thought of actors like Peter Ustinov and Robert Morley.

'As it happened, Eric was being filmed at the time by Anglia Television having his portrait done. Someone at Anglia then suggested Eric Morecambe. This kind of wrong-footed me as it was so completely different from what I'd had in mind. In fact I would confess to you now that I wasn't terribly positive about the idea.

'The head of production took me to one side and said that if I could get Eric Morecambe then I must do so, because there was no one bigger.

'I tracked Eric down, telephoned him and explained that the film, a short, would be called *Betjeman's Britain,* and would he remotely be interested. Straight off he said, "Yes, fine!" In fact, I got the immediate impression he was very up for something different from the Morecambe and Wise format.'

This is something I know to be accurate from conversations I'd had with my father at this time. In fact as early as 1973 he had been saying that he felt Morecambe and Wise were getting themselves in a bit of a rut.

'As I recall,' continued Charles, 'he came over for filming the afternoon before. We had dinner and a bit of a chat together, and filmed the next day and he went home. Just as he was leaving he came back to me and said, "Sunshine! If there's anything you ever want me to do, just give me a call." I smiled on the outside, but was thinking, "Shit! I've got the biggest star on television and he wants to work on anything I can offer him." But what came out my mouth was, "What do you feel you'd *like* to do?" And he replied, "Do you know, I've always wanted to do something about ghosts!"'

'The only thing that the film and TV people wanted was Morecambe and Wise, and they didn't want anything that detracted from that.'

Hearing this from Charles triggered a memory of Eric standing in front of his mirror in the hallway of his house saying he would love to write a ghost story about a spectral life inside a mirror.

'He was serious,' said Charles. 'I mean he wanted to do it for real as a straight bit of acting – no comedy stuff. And I was pretty interested in the subject, and understood the line he wanted to take. It would be completely different from Morecambe and Wise, and that would have given me as much pleasure as it would have done Eric. I was understandably buoyed up about this. But could I get anyone interested? Not a chance! The only thing that the film and TV people wanted was Morecambe and Wise, and they didn't want anything that detracted from that.'

'That mentality of playing it safe was creeping in around this time as the more adventurous programme makers of the fifties and sixties retired or died.'

This was something Eric and Ernie experienced when they moved from the BBC to Thames Television in the late seventies. In essence Thames wanted the same shows the BBC had given viewers during the previous decade, and that despite the stars wanting to develop in other areas of their comedy work. For instance, both Eric and Ernie were keen to pursue the idea of a Morecambe and Wise series which had none of the variety guest stars, duologue in front of the curtains, and other familiar elements, but took place entirely in their make-believe flat and bedroom. At the time the flat and the bedroom represented about twelve minutes of their shows, so the idea was to make them into a sit-com that was quietly announcing itself along the lines of 'You've seen short moments from our life in the flat and the bedroom, now here's a series just of those elements.' I, for one, encouraged him to push on this as I thought it was a great idea. But as Charles found out himself, no one was interested – even when it was Eric Morecambe making the suggestion.

'Making the odd little cameo in a twenty-two-minute TV or cinema short,

or having his portrait painted on Anglia TV, was acceptable at a push, but that was it,' said Charles. 'Any thought of a new direction seemed to imply there was an element of risk as far as the powers that be at that time were concerned – the risk of killing the goose that laid the golden egg.

'That mentality of playing it safe was creeping in around this time as the more adventurous programme makers of the fifties and sixties retired or died, and this new breed of programme makers came in. Even today there is a playing-it-safe feel to much of the programming we see.

'But with Eric at least we were able to go on to film another Betjeman short,' explained Charles. 'Paramount Pictures had seen the original one, loved it, and asked if I would do something for them. Being a prat I went and offered them another Betjeman instead of taking advantage of doing something totally new. As it happened, the second Betjeman with Eric worked incredibly well. Eric played an army major in the film. The poem was called "Invasion Exercise on the Poultry Farm". We got Susannah York and Beryl Reid involved as it was a kind of take on the movie *The Killing of Sister George*, in which Beryl had starred some years earlier.

'In the Betjeman poem a paratrooper lands off course in the countryside. Susannah's character takes a fancy to him and goes off with him. Beryl rings up the local military base and demands someone comes along [Eric] to deal with the wayward paratrooper. Instead, Eric's character goes off with Susannah, leaving the paratrooper tied up.

'It was fine – in fact it was good – but for me personally it felt too like the original film we'd shot a year earlier. What I should have done was something a bit more adventurous. However, it proved the most successful cinema short ever. The head of UIP thought it was just wonderful, and he put it out with everything, including the latest Bond movie of the day and *Raiders of the Lost Ark*.

'What was pleasing for me, and no doubt Eric, was that short films are something everyone tends to avoid, but with this one they actually advertised it. It went out as "*Late Flowering Love* starring Eric Morecambe!" They knew that would get the punters in on Eric's name.'

After filming was over, Eric joked with Charles as he left, 'Same time next year, sunshine?' Charles was up for that, especially as the second Betjeman had gone down so well, including a double-page spread in a national tabloid.

'But a year later I still hadn't managed to get anything together,' said Charles, 'probably because this time I really was keen to do something entirely different from the two Betjeman films. Soon, though, the idea of what would be *The Passionate Pilgrim* started to formulate in my head. The structure of the piece was to tell a story in three or four parts. It was all to be set around this eccentric lord in a castle – that being Eric, of course – trying to woo this very attractive damsel – who would be played by Madeline Smith – and this strapping knight trying to beat him to the damsel – finally played by actor Tom Baker.'

Interestingly, Tom Baker hadn't been first choice for Charles. 'Originally the role played by Tom Baker was to be played by Sean Connery,' he told me, which came as a big surprise as I had no previous knowledge of this. 'Eric and Sean couldn't match availability, and time was pressing and we needed to move on with the project, so I approached Tom Baker.'

Tom Baker, of course, is famous around the world as the fourth incarnation of the Gallifreyan with the keys to the *Tardis*, the Doctor, in the BBC's *Doctor Who*.

Although I knew Eric and Tom had met some five years before the film and that they went on to make this film together, my knowledge till now had gone no further. Mind you, I knew that Tom Baker has a certain reputation for not being the easiest on-set actor to ever appear in front of a camera, yet, accord-

Eric with co-star Tom Baker on location for Charles Wallace's film The Passionate Pilgrim.

ing to Charles, 'he was on his best behaviour. Tom was in awe of Eric Morecambe, and felt genuinely honoured to be working with him in this three-han-
der – Eric, Tom, and Madeline Smith.

'There was only one time, when Eric wasn't there, that Tom got a bit
grumpy. But even then, with Eric's energy on the set, Tom was not going to be
difficult. Also Tom had seen how compliant Eric was, always willing to do whatever the director, me, wanted to do. It should also be pointed out that when I
approached Tom to do the part, he said, "To be honest I'd never heard of you, but
if Eric Morecambe has agreed to do it, then that's good enough for me!"'

'Eric wasn't that accustomed to being without Ernie Wise, in whom he perhaps had the greatest straight man who had ever breathed.'

With some irony I sense that Tom Baker's expression almost cues the
moment from *The Morecambe and Wise Show* when Eric, on hearing Ernie say
similar words, turns to the camera, and effectively to the viewer at home, and
says, 'This boy's a fool!'

'Eric, who liked Tom enormously,' continued Charles, 'wasn't that accustomed to being without Ernie Wise, in whom he perhaps had the greatest
straight man who had ever breathed. Sure, he could have little digs at Ernie, as
partners always do, but you knew without a shadow of a doubt that he had a
great love for him and a great loyalty to him. I think he also sensed that without
his own contribution what would Ernie be able to do? And that probably is the
sad truth of being regarded as the straight man in a double act.

'Working with Tom Baker reaffirmed Eric's understanding of how wonderful Ernie was as a straight man,' Charles asserted. 'Eric did say to me in the middle of filming *The Passionate Pilgrim* that working with Tom was like working with

a piece of wood. "I love Tom, but I don't get anything back from him." Tom, as Eric knew full well, was a brilliant actor, but he's not a stand-up comedy type. And that was Eric's problem within the confines of the piece we were making.

'Of course, Eric was so used to working with Ernie for over forty years by now, and almost to the exclusion of anyone else, that they had this rapport which had never failed them. You put Eric with someone who is a brilliant actor but not that type of natural comedy expert and it's going to be tough.'

Charles explained his inspiration for this surreal short film with its double entendres. 'As a kid I was, and still am in adulthood, a great fan of Tom and Jerry cartoons. I saw the basis of their relationship as the basis of Eric's and Tom's in *The Passionate Pilgrim,* and with Madeline Smith as a sort of Tweety Pie [the little canary-like bird that appeared in many cartoon films with Sylvester the cat] character.'

A rather bizarre, quirky little number, and with a *Carry On*-style narration by the late John Le Mesurier, *The Passionate Pilgrim* has something very naive and lovable about it. Whether this effect is enhanced by the knowledge that it was Eric's very last piece of work is hard to know. But it has a genuine fairytale quality and it is a great pity that fate made it impossible to be completed in the manner wanted by Charles Wallace.

Charles began talking me through the process of what he originally wanted to achieve with the film. 'The plan was to do three or four connected stories. Each segment, or episode, would star Eric as the lord, Tom as the arch-rival and a different girl – Madeline Smith being the first – as the one both men are trying to woo. These wouldn't go out as individual films, but as one short film combining the three episodes.

'I decided that the best way forward would be to shoot the first segment of *The Passionate Pilgrim,* show it to the right people, and then the money would come in for us to complete the other two segments and the film would be complete. The first segment, which was to end up being the whole film in the end, was shot as an historic piece at Hever Castle in Kent. I put it together roughly and showed it to various people, but unlike the Betjeman[-narrated] films I just couldn't get the financial backing, which struck me as ridiculous. Eric rang me up: "How's it going, sunshine?" Well, I didn't have the guts to tell him I wasn't getting anywhere with it. Also, I knew it would work – it was a great project with Eric starring. It was a guaranteed success. Feeling pretty certain therefore that all would come right in the end, we went ahead and started shooting the third segment of the story, planning to return to do the second segment later to finish the film off.

'Again it was Eric and Tom, but by this time Tom was no longer a knight but a postman on a bicycle, and Eric was still the local lord, but now dressed in keeping with the much later times of our setting.

'I was still under a lot of pressure, and I was only continuing filming to keep Eric on board. If I'd had to go to him and say I wasn't able to get it together, he'd understandably have felt uncomfortable and reckon he'd backed a loser!'

Some of the filming was done back at Hever Castle. After that there came a long break as Charles tried to raise funds. He did so, but not in the manner he had planned. Tough times call for tough measures, it seems. 'I sold my flat in the meantime, bought a house, got a whacking great mortgage, so I had the funding in place to get at least another day's filming in the can.

'By now another year had gone – 1983 had become '84 – and I knew I just had to keep Eric there with me, and I was sure that eventually we'd get the thing completed.

'The following Sunday, Eric was dead.'

'Then a slightly eerie thing happened. We were set to do another day's filming, which would have basically finished the segment with Tom as the postman. We had Beryl Reid lined up to play Eric's mother.

'We had lined it up that we were going to shoot on a particular Wednesday – just with Eric and Beryl Reid and the new damsel, as Tom's stuff was now all in the can. However, during the previous week I felt I didn't have things totally together enough to shoot that day. I rang Eric up just to let him know, and to make sure he wouldn't mind that we were putting back shooting until the following week. Eric was the easiest person to work with, and I thought therefore he would just say it was fine – no problem. And in this plaintive voice he said, "Oh! Do we really have to?" "Crumbs," thought I. "I must've upset him somehow." Eventually he said, "Well, if you really have to change it I suppose I can go and mow the lawn instead." I hung up with this conversation nagging at me, because it was so unlike Eric to be that fussed by a week's delay.

'The following Sunday, Eric was dead.'

'I cannot help but think Eric had an inclination that things weren't right: a premonition that time was short, and that was why he wanted to finish the film.'

My father was very perceptive about his health, and all his close family felt with hindsight that at this time he was having quite a few premonitions. He was giving belongings away, like pipes and books, sorting out his photo albums and his office, and generally distancing himself from everyday mortal existence. And, looking back, Charles Wallace concluded the same.

'I cannot help but think Eric had an inclination that things weren't right: a premonition that time was short, and *that* was why he wanted to finish the film.

'On the other hand, and from my own perspective, I'm rather glad we didn't do that last day's filming. It would have been very strenuous for him, and in light of what soon happened to him, I would have felt terribly guilty that it was the effort required to film that had brought on the fatal heart attack. I was happy to live without the thought that I was the man who killed Eric Morecambe!'

I suggested to Charles that it must have been a big shock for all the others involved in the project when it was announced that Eric had died. He replied,

'To be honest, it was such a big shock to *me* that I didn't really have the time or inclination to think about how the others might be affected, beyond his family, of course.'

With Charles left with an incomplete third episode, a second episode that hadn't even been fully written, and only a first episode complete, what would be the new plan for *The Passionate Pilgrim*? Too much time and money had been invested to just shrug shoulders and walk away.

'The first part that we had in the can eventually went out as a cinema short as the complete story of *The Passionate Pilgrim*,' explains Charles. 'It was only released in cinemas in the UK and again went out with a James Bond movie, and *again* it was advertised everywhere on the back of the name Eric Morecambe.'

As I was leaving, Charles was clearly keen to impart to me a few further thoughts about my father. 'The only real chance of Eric branching out and displaying his full potential would have been if Ernie had gone first. Awful thing to say, but it's true. I know Eric wouldn't have done to Ernie what Dud [Dudley

Moore] did to Pete [Peter Cook] – though that relationship was obviously more stressed. It didn't mean Eric was any less keen to branch out. His view of Morecambe and Wise, as he explained it to me, was that he wanted to keep it going as long as possible, particularly because of Ernie. However, he felt they'd done all they could with the series, and it was increasingly becoming a strain to keep the standard up. Again it was this idea he had of "duty to the fans" – that desire to keep the people laughing – that drove him ever onwards.

'Even when people were with him whom he knew well – indeed me while we were filming – he felt this need to entertain. But he didn't *have* to for our benefit, he just felt he should.

'Mind you, my girlfriend of the time often tells me how once she was driving Eric between locations and couldn't find her driving glasses. Quick as a flash Eric quipped, "What you need is a prescription windscreen."'

The last recorded work of Morecambe and Wise was their 1984 film *Night Train to Murder*. This was supposed to be the film that would not only be their first big-screen release since 1967 but eclipse that trio of Rank movies made back in the mid-sixties. But it was truly poor, if not awful.

Actress Lysette Anthony was a very young actress back in 1984 when she was hired to play alongside Eric and Ernie as Eric's niece in this sub-standard Agatha Christie-style murder drama. 'We laughed and laughed and had such a great time making the film,' she told me. 'Even between takes the laughter went on, but nobody pointed out, perhaps because we were all having such a fun time, that the script was very thin and didn't really work.'

I find Lysette's observation interesting as it sort of confirms a niggling thought of my own which has been growing over the years: that Thames used its Euston Films arm to lure Eric and Ernie to take *The Morecambe and Wise Show* to Thames Television, but with no real intent to expend energy and talent on trying to make the film a big success.

What was surprising was that my father was unable to see beyond the merriment and realize he was involved in a duff project. It was only at the screening of the film that the horror of what they had done – for that was his opinion – was fully understood. As a wholly professional performer with fantastic perception and understanding of Morecambe and Wise, he was more gutted by his own failure to pick up on the failings at the time of filming than anything else.

Lysette Anthony did point out to me that everyone at least enjoyed the whole process. 'Your father was one of the kindest people I've ever met, let alone work with. I was going through a really rough time on the domestic front while filming, and your father sensed things weren't right, though I'd told him nothing. He was terribly protective of me.

'He was a lovely, decent, very silly, naughty, gorgeous man. I still have a real soft spot for him.'

Lysette was surprised at the difference between Eric and Ernie. 'With Morecambe and Wise,' she explained, 'when you met Eric it was exactly what you wanted and expected him to be: he was *that* funny and generous as both comedian and person. Brightening people's day was very much at the core of his being. And with Ernie it was much less so. And that was a shock. Ernie was quite cold and very much more cautious with people on the set. Together, as a partnership, they were brilliant, of course, and Eric is beyond being an icon and deserves to be so. When I work with other great actors and comedians and let slip I worked on a film with Morecambe and Wise, they are both flummoxed and in awe, such is the reputation of their double act.'

Alongside Lysette Anthony and Eric and Ernie themselves were actors such as Fulton Mackay, best known for his role as the prison warder in Ronnie Barker's *Porridge*. But it wasn't enough to save this project.

After the private screening of the film, and when Eric was able to put a coherent sentence together, the first thing he requested was that the project be shelved. He was told it was impossible to do that.

As it happened, Eric would be dead within a few weeks, and as a mark of respect for his wishes, while not shelving the film altogether, Thames did not give it its theatrical release, finally screening it on TV in a children's programming slot. How ironic that Morecambe and Wise were seduced to Thames from the BBC by the promise of a 'big film'. And doubly ironic is the fact that the film has benefited from both video and DVD release, including international sales, proving quite popular in countries where Eric and Ernie were virtually or completely unknown.

Paul Merton told me an interesting story about the move to Thames. 'I bumped into [the BBC's] former Head of Light Entertainment, Bill Cotton, at Waterloo Station a while ago. We got to talking about Morecambe and Wise, and he told me that Eric had gone to the bar of the BBC for a drink during the last Christmas he was alive. Bill Cotton had been there too, and in conversation Bill had encouraged him and Ernie to return to the BBC. He did this because he inferred from Eric's comments that all was not quite as it should have been at Thames; that the move to the different studio was more negative than positive. As it is we'll never know what might have happened. Eric died the following May. But it's interesting to imagine their return to the BBC and to see them possibly taking the Morecambe and Wise format even further.'

'Brightening people's day was very much at the core of his being.'

Michael Parkinson told me, 'I don't think Bill Cotton ever recovered from Morecambe and Wise leaving the BBC. He was devastated. Heartbroken.

'Eric and Ernie had to make a decision for what they saw as best for them, but Bill took it very personally. I'd go and see Bill around 5pm at the close of play as it were. He was having personal difficulties much of the time back then as well, but he'd always come back to go on about why Eric and Ernie had left. But they never fell out with each other over it. It was more that Bill couldn't come to terms with it. But he never stopped loving them as people and performers and would have taken them back at the drop of a hat.

'There was no greater champion for Morecambe and Wise right from the very beginning.'

Curtain Call

*'All comedians are supposed to want to play Hamlet, I know, but that's not me. I was offered Bottom by the BBC a couple of weeks ago – the part of Bottom, that is – in **A Midsummer Night's Dream**. But I had to turn it down. I couldn't learn all those lines, for one thing.'*

Eric and Ernie presented with a framed award. This still hangs on the wall of what was Eric's study. The study was the subject of a Channel 4 documentary in 2004.

We all secretly know, but choose to forget, that anything that represents true happiness has to come from within. 'Though we travel the world over to find the beautiful, we must carry it within us or find it not,' wrote Ralph Waldo Emerson. And I think 'the beautiful' can easily be exchanged for 'happiness' in that context. Our desire to add externally – materially – to ourselves in an attempt to feel more complete has never worked. So is seeking celebrity status the last desperate attempt to escape reality? If that is the case, then the problem is worse than it appears. All I know for sure is that you only have to look at the famous clientele in the expensive rehab clinics and ask yourself, are they there because they are happy? My father had the fame but could separate himself from the illusion it somehow made him special.

An interview I did with my father in 1982 gives a brief insight into his personality and disciplined manner; how he was the antithesis of the celebrity notion of today.

> ME: *Is there anyone in particular in the music world that you have not met and would wish to meet?*
>
> ERIC: *Not individually, no. I have met many of the ones I consider great. André Previn, Yehudi Menuhin and so on. Perhaps I am accustomed to it, but it is no big thrill in meeting them as, like myself, they are ordinary people. I believe that it is the ones with the lesser talent who try to be something they are not: they go a little round the twist in the end. Anyone who can't handle it shouldn't be allowed it; sex included.*

Morecambe and Wise were not celebrities *per se,* so what makes them continue to be so loved today is possibly less to do with imagery and more to do with the content of their work and the nature of their relationship. Morecambe and Wise didn't tell jokes. Jokes can date performers. Satire, which arguably is the sharpest form of wit, is dated almost the day after it's been aired, as its content is based on the news and political personalities of the current moment. You have a change of prime minister and/or government, or a new story or scandal hits the headlines, and the material is instantly old and woefully unfunny. Perhaps if left long enough – like the satirical wit of Saki (Hector Munro) from the early part of the twentieth century – it develops a kind of retro edge to it. But relatively contemporary material, like that of *Not the Nine O'Clock News* – the vehicle which launched Rowan Atkinson, Mel Smith, Griff Rhys Jones, and Pamela Stephenson's careers – is an example of shelf-life comedy. Hugely popular at its zenith in the late seventies and eighties, it is now hardly even mentioned when comedy is discussed. I remember being at Rowan Atkinson's house in the eighties, shortly after the series had finished, and he could hardly bear to talk about it, let alone watch any of it.

But Morecambe and Wise didn't do satire – they didn't even tell jokes. What they did was share with the public their intimacy and the relationship that had been constantly developing from their early variety-hall days – which were beautifully studied in William Cook's 2007 book *Morecambe and Wise Untold* – through to their spectacular BBC Christmas shows. The humour was effortlessly grounded in a genuine shared history, as these two giants of comedy had indeed trod the boards together as young lads, travelling to work from Scotland down to the south coast of England and back.

Eric once wrote, 'Ours is a relationship based on genuine friendship and a mutual admiration. We both think the other is the funniest man breathing!'

Ant and Dec perhaps exist in a time where a decent vehicle for their talents is lacking, and perhaps a closer match to Morecambe and Wise from the current crop would be Mitchell and Webb, who fully began to realize their potential through the series *Peep Show*. What makes the comparison particularly apt is that Mitchell and Webb have a real outlet for their talent in the format of their shows, rather than messing around with would-be celebrities, real celebrities, or involving the public at large.

I sense that some of the current purveyors of our entertainment recognize they are overly valued: certainly Ricky Gervais, when interviewed on a TV chat show, said he was excessively rewarded for what he did. And Ant and Dec told me that they were flattered by any comparisons to Eric and Ernie, but wouldn't go near making such an assumption themselves. And being a genuine 'star' demands more than being nice, extrovert, and smiley, or my local butcher should get BAFTAs and ridiculously large pay cheques.

Fundamentally there's a 'flavour of the month' feel to entertainers these days that didn't exist a generation or two ago. Instead of years of hard slog and having to constantly prove your worth, there seems to be an element of 'These

two are well known and well liked – get 'em another award and a few more million quid, and in a couple of years we'll find a replacement for them.'

A journalist writing a profile of my father used the following words to
describe him: 'Eric Morecambe was the rarest of things: a universally popular
mainstream comedian who also commands respect from critics and alternative
comics (see his virtual clone Vic Reeves).'

That's probably spot on, though it should be added that the biggest reason
Eric is so broadly accepted is because he was a thoroughly decent human being.
You can't fake that. Some have tried, and it's not my job to name names – there
are plenty you can come up with yourselves if you ponder a moment. But with
Eric – *and* Ernie – it was clearly genuine: they wanted to entertain and they
were affable with it.

Peter Kay, who arrived as a solo stand-up comedian for the most part and
developed into a gifted comic actor, does have that timelessness about him. His

comedy is not dissimilar to that of Morecambe and Wise. Peter often reminds me of my father in the way he uses his voice and in his movement. They both hail from Lancashire – well, Kay is from Bolton, which although now part of Greater Manchester is still Lancs in most people's minds – and he retains the lovable sincerity that Eric possessed – he is an observer of life, not a purveyor of a string of one-liners. Like Eric bickering with Ernie over which of them their school teacher liked best and who had the best pair of shoes when they were kids forty years earlier, Kay will recall bonfire nights in his back garden at home, and which biscuits fall apart quickest when dunked in a mug of tea (or brew, as he calls it).

With Kay I always sense that, like Eric, he would be happy to entertain a crowd in his kitchen at home for nothing, if that is what it took for him to perform. His comedic skills are possibly on a par with those of the late, great Ronnie Barker.

'The problem I have with today's comedians,' says Michael Parkinson, 'is they're not funny! Funny is what you get with Eric and Ernie and Tommy Cooper and Les Dawson. With the exception of Peter Kay, who to all intents and purposes is old-school in his style of comedy, you don't see that now. Possibly Lee Evans has something, too. But Peter has clearly been influenced by Eric and that adds to his likeability: he brings yesteryear to today and it's wonderful.'

Ricky Gervais has elements in his comic persona of both Eric *and* Ernie. When in character, like Ernie he can be rather bumptious and forthright and a little full of his own supposed talent and importance – writer Eddie Braben's device of creating Ernie as the frustrated playwright in *The Morecambe and Wise Show* being a good illustration of that. At other times Gervais can be like Eric in his mischievousness and gentle naivety. In his series *Extras* he takes a very popular Morecambe and Wise theme – the appearance and use of a guest star on the show. Ricky uses his guest stars more aggressively – some are lampooned hilariously, while others are made to appear downright evil! – but essentially it is still Morecambe and Wise in its execution. And it is brilliant. When interviewed

on TV, Gervais's colleague Stephen Merchant described *Extras* as 'The classic Morecambe and Wise device'.

During an interview of his own Gervais talked a bit about Eric's comedy brain. He gave an excellent example of Eric's irrepressible wit when he mentioned the footage of my father leaving hospital surrounded by the media after his second heart attack. As Eric, led by my mother, attempts to get away from the hospital porch to his car, one reporter asks, 'Will you take it easy for a bit?' Eric, without missing a beat, replies, 'If I can get a bit, I'll take it easy!'

As Gervais points out, this quick-wittedness follows an extreme life-threatening health scare. For me it illuminates the world my father inhabited: the constant obligation he felt – real or imagined – to look for the amusing. As I've

Eric, Joan and Gail at the Morecambe home. This was one of a series of photos for a magazine, and you can tell by Gail's expression that we're building up to a 'You'll miss me when I'm gone' moment from Eric! She's clearly trying her very best not to laugh at what he's just said.

said in interviews, he wasn't someone who woke up in the morning thinking of what he might like for breakfast; he awoke thinking what humour he might find and use in the day ahead. And that was part of his gift for comedy.

Rowan Atkinson is a brilliant comic who has proved time and again over several decades that sheer talent runs from every pore in his body. Spike Milligan, Peter Sellers, Peter Cook, Tommy Cooper, Charlie Chaplin, Groucho Marx, and many others are genuine comic masters whose work, pain, and talent likewise spans decades. I know comedy is subjective – what one person finds funny another might not – but there is an acceptable criterion when it comes to using the word 'genius', and in my view there are very few of those performing comedy out there today who deserve to be described as possessing it: and when the media proclaims they are geniuses, we all should feel vaguely uncomfortable for not questioning it, as the media often has its own agenda.

It's while in conversation with Michael Parkinson that I realise how much he appreciated Eric's pure humour – the comedian who always remained a decent and unaffected human being. He said, 'Eric and I couldn't be described as having been close friends or anything like that, but we really enjoyed each other's company. 'We'd go out to restaurants and in Eric's own gentle way he'd cause complete turmoil. The waiter would come up talk to him and Eric would look the wrong side. Hilarious stuff, but what is it with these great comics that they just can't switch off.'

In conversation with my mother for this book, she told me an interesting thing I'd never before heard. Apparently in the early seventies a Dutch double act approached Eric and Ernie to say that they enjoyed their shows so much they were going to use their material. People weren't that copyright-conscious back then; certainly not Eric and Ernie, who seemed to find the whole thing vaguely entertaining. 'I think they arranged to meet up with your dad and Ernie,' said my mother. 'Whether that happened or not, I can't recall, but they received an envelope with a handful of [bank]notes in it – a pittance for the material they were using, of course. But it was very amusing. I think I've still got the notes somewhere!'

Since Eric's death I've always kept half an eye on new comedians emerging who clearly have been influenced by Morecambe and Wise. The latest one to grab my attention is the hugely talented Lee Mack, whom I first saw on Jack Dee's live show broadcast from the Apollo Theatre in London. He's the first comedian in a long, long time to really press my buttons, and the fact that during his act he effortlessly glides into an Eric impression without ever really saying he's doing it, no doubt helps.

'Doing the comedy circuit,' says Lee, 'you're always asked who your favourite comics are, and the two names which always crop up are Eric Morecambe and Stan Laurel.

'I used to think it was so important in my life to make a decision as to which of them I thought was funniest. I'd spend hours on long journeys contemplating this.'

I pointed out to Lee that it's funny the way kids can think like that. A twinkle appeared in his eye as he said, 'Kid? This was two years ago on my way to gigs!'

He settled on Eric as his all-time comic hero because of his longevity. 'Longevity in this business is so special, remarkable and, once acquired, permanent by its nature. But if you said back in the mid-1980s that your favourite comedians were Morecambe and Wise, you'd have got strange looks. It was the era of the alternatives, and the immediate past comedians suffered more than the black and white ones of the 1920s who were revered as high art. Frankie Howerd, Tommy Cooper, Cannon and Ball, Benny Hill, Les Dawson and Morecambe and Wise were out of favour. Yet look at Morecambe and Wise now all these years on.'

In my father's last days, as they turned out to be, he made an interesting observation which initially shocked me but on reflection sort of demonstrates what forty-three years of *any* partnership can create. 'If Ern and I stay together and carry on making shows for the foreseeable future,' he told me, 'then I'm going to end up hating him, and he's going to end up hating me. It has to be that way:

it's too long to be doing the same thing. All the little faults and irritations will become massive and destroy us. I wouldn't want that.'

As someone who has doggedly analysed his father for twenty-five years, I constantly racked my brains while writing this book to make sure that he made no other observation or suggestion immediately before or after this comment, and that my declining memory is recalling things with 100 per cent accuracy. The reason for my thoroughness is that although it would have been natural for him to have added 'therefore we must stop doing Morecambe and Wise shows', he genuinely didn't. I've *imagined* that he went on to say that, but I know that he just smiled and walked out the living room, bringing to a close one of the occasional yet enlightening conversations we were prone to, especially in the last months of his life for some reason. None of it was to matter, of course, because

1979, and Eric's return from hospital following heart surgery. Ernie joins his partner in the Morecambe garden, the first get-together since the operation, hence these press photos. Fortunately, the moustache went the next day!

within a fortnight he was dead. Death overcame all considerations, including what might have been.

My father died suddenly on 28 May 1984 in the wings of a theatre in Tewkesbury, Gloucestershire. He had being doing a solo show – a Q&A for his old friend and former variety-hall stalwart Stan Stennett – during which he covered the many aspects and times of his remarkable life. Strange really that he should have gone over his whole life story and then died at the completion of its telling.

I think he recognized very profoundly that everything about this physical existence was transient, and possibly not as important as we like to think – or that we're not as important as we like to think we are within it. We certainly can't take anything with us when we leave, which makes a mockery of the idea of ownership. My father's entire fame – the attention, the money, the plaudits, and even the illnesses – were rendered meaningless, and he knew that was how it would be. He also knew that it was OK: so long as we, in some familial gesture, continued to watch the shows, then all else was fine.

During our many walks across the fields at the back of his house we would talk about the books we both wanted to one day write. Although the fact that both he and I were keen to write could be a thorny issue between us at times, it was a subject never avoided. Actually my father never avoided *anything* if it was there to be discussed. Without any direct connection to the books we were talking about, he said, quite suddenly and almost dismissively, 'You can write what you like about me when I'm dead and gone.' What struck me – and at this particularly juncture I had no plans to write anything at all about him – was that he really meant it. It was said in that 'It's not going to be *my* problem' kind of way. That conversation made me start to evaluate many things in my own existence. If this man with all the trappings of success following a huge and at times very hard career could evaluate it with a half-smile and a dismissive shrug, then what was there really to worry about? None of it, of course, is that important beyond the importance we allow ourselves to imagine.

Paradoxically, I sensed that my father hid behind the trappings of fame, and behind the material rewards and comforts it had brought him. I'm sure this reaction was fear-based, and it was certainly contradictory to those moments I've just described. While accepting that his mortal life was a blink of the eye in the history of humankind on our planet, he still was comforted by having things he couldn't have had as a kid, and equally fearful they might be taken away. In several conversations with my mother when they were discussing the purchase of something one would hear him say, 'Can we afford it?'

I'm so thankful he never took himself or his image too seriously (unlike many from his own era and the current era that I've stumbled across). And when you consider how fêted, how loved and adored by a vast public he was and remarkably still is, it is truly admirable that he resisted believing the myth of his worth.

Ernie Wise died of heart failure on 21 March 1999 after several years of ill-health. A couple of minor strokes and two heart attacks had left his memory impaired. Personally I found this very tragic, considering his enthusiasm and effervescence of just a few years earlier, during which I'd had the opportunity to meet up with him on several occasions, mostly to discuss work on what would one day become *The Play What I Wrote*.

Ernie's passing was the final chapter in a long and entertaining story: two boys who had dreamed of one day becoming big stars, but who never really believed it was likely to happen: that was how Ernie once described it.

The polished, clog-dancing discovery Ernie Wise that fate had brought together with the singing, all-round entertainer Eric Bartholomew had gone to join his partner – at least that's how the media depicted it in both words and cartoon. Having to accept that the story really was now over was one of the hardest things to take on board. While Ernie had been alive the double act sort of still existed as a living entity.

The years have ticked by. As well as this being Eric's twenty-fifth anniversary, it is also Ernie's tenth, and I'm sure this book will be only one of many celebrations to mark the passing of both of these giants.

Reminiscing with my mother not long ago about Eric, I told her how sad and frustrating I felt it was that my father, while reaching the top of his profession, had been allowed so little time to enjoy it; that mostly he had been on the journey getting there. But my mother saw it differently. 'Since his first heart attack,' she told me, 'your dad understood that every breath he took could have been his last. Nearly dying at forty-two gave him a sharper sense of the moment, and the recognition that it must be enjoyed.' And she added, 'As well as living more in the moment, he would also tell me with genuine delight what a wonderful life he had lived; that there should be no regrets if anything happened to him.'

As for Morecambe and Wise the industry, this still appears to tick on. At the time of writing this book, as well as the documentaries and various TV film projects under discussion concerning both of them, I am also in discussion with the local MP in Lancaster about setting up an Eric Morecambe museum in Morecambe. This excites me greatly, as there is no better place for all the various bits of memorabilia to be displayed for the benefit of the visiting tourists and local people.

As with Laurel and Hardy before them, as the years pass by there will be ever fewer who can recall them as a living act. Slowly, therefore, Eric and Ernie will be become a part of our psyche – two familiar names and faces that instantaneously conjure up an image of brilliance combined with daftness, and will guarantee a smile on everyone's face for generations to come.

That's not a bad legacy.

Even today people say to me that they can't believe Eric has gone. I just point out that by now he is returned – reincarnated and probably sitting in some classroom, unaware of his previous life, yet biding his time before letting his comic mayhem run riot again.

Two of a Kind

Two of a kind,
For your information,
We're two of a kind.

Two of a kind,
It's my observation,
We're two of a kind.

Just like peas in a pod,
Birds of a feather,
Alone or together, you'll find.

That we are two ...
Two of a kind.

PART TWO

Wit and Wisdom

In Eric and Ernie's Words

An Extract from 'Morecambe and Wise in "Double Trouble"'

NUMBER TWO

MORECAMBE and WISE

in

"DOUBLE TROUBLE"

with

Deryck Guyler

Hattie Jacques

Sidney Tafler

Herbert Smith

BBC Northern Variety Orchestra
conducted by Alyn Ainsworth

Incidental music by Alan Roper

Script by Frank Roscoe & Cass James

Produced by John Ammonds

(from the Playhouse Theatre, Manchester)

NEHS: Wednesday, October 26, 1955: 7.00 - 7.30 p.m.

Pre-recorded: Sunday, October 23: 8.00-8.45 p.m. on TLS 7034

Rehearsal 3.00 p.m.

CONTINUITY: This is the North of England Home Service.

1   (F/X Street noises as "In Town Tonight")
                     CUE LIGHT.

2   ERNIE: Stop!!!

3   (F/X Street noises stop abruptly)

4   ERNIE: Once again we stop the roar of London's traffic...
                Wait a minute!   This isn't In Town Tonight!   Why
                are we stopping the traffic?

5   ERIC: My Grannie wants to cross the road!!

6   GRAMS: OPENING THEME MUSIC

7   ROGER: (over music) Yes, ladies and gentlemen ... it's
                those two Demon Blunderers of Fleet Street ...
                ERIC   ERNIE
                Morecambe and Wise in Double Trouble!!

8   GRAMS: BRING UP MUSIC THEN FADE

9   ROGER: We should like to take you to the Editor's office
                of that famous newspaper, The Morning Sun ...
                where you can hear the Editor talking to his Star
                Reporter, Ernie Wise, who is of course only Wise
                because Morecambe is so stupid .....

                        (FADE INTO)

10 DERYCK: So that's the assignment Wise.   I want you to go
                to the village of Peacehaven on Dartmoor and get a
                complete and exclusive story on this invention of
                Professor Boniface.   I'm warning you, it'll be a
                tough job because he can't stand reporters and he's
                heavily guarded.

1   ERNIE: I understand Mr. Crossman ... and you say no one has any idea what his invention is.

2   DERYCK: None at all, but it must be something big because some American scientist is coming over to see it.

3   ERNIE: Don't worry Mr. Crossman. Morecambe and I will get that story even if he has to die in the attempt!

4   DERYCK: Morecambe!! That incompetent bungler! Last week I asked him for a story about the navy, and he wrote the one about what the actress said to the sailor! Why on earth do you want to take him with you?

5   ERNIE: Well, I promised his mother I'd make his father proud of him. You see, his father was disappointed when Eric was born.

6   DERYCK: I suppose his father wanted a girl.

7   ERNIE: No - he wanted a boy.

8   DERYCK: Well, as soon as you've made all the arrangements, go and collect Morecambe and get started for Peacehaven. He's probably still trying to answer last week's mail ....

(CROSS FADE)

9   HATTIE: And here's a letter from a young man who writes "I work in a Drapery Store, and have fallen in love with one of the customers. I have tried to get her interested by giving her presents - so far I've given her a length of satin and a piece of tweed, but I still haven't made any headway. What else should I try?"

1 ERIC: Dear Sir.   Try a bit of flannel!

          (Applause)

2 ERIC: Just end the letter in the usual way - "Yours
             sincerely, Auntie Ethel!"

3 HATTIE: Oh Mr. Morecambe!   You're wonderful!   You're
             the best Auntie Ethel we've ever had!!   I thought
             Mrs. Fleming was good until you took over.   But
             you're different from her!

4 ERIC: You've been looking at my laundry list!

5 HATTIE: It's wonderful the way you bring young people
             together.

6 ERIC: Oh, I'm not as good as my brother;   he's brought
             more young people together than any man alive!

7 HATTIE: Does he give advice as well?

8 ERIC: No - he invented the Creep.

9 HATTIE: Mr. Morecambe ... Eric ... you're so handsome.
             Just looking at you makes me feel lovesick.

10 ERIC: Miss Lightbody!   Cut out the love in office hours.

11 HATTIE: All right ... just looking at you makes me feel
             sick!

12 ERIC: That's better!   Now let's get to work.

13 HATTIE: Right - kiss me!

14 ERIC: Please......I never kiss girls when I'm smoking.

15 HATTIE: But you're not smoking!!

1 ERIC: Got a match?

2 HATTIE: Don't you want my lips?   Last night a man told
me he'd give anything for them.

3 ERIC: Who was he - a glass-blower?

4 HATTIE: Well really!!!   Just for that I'll go out tonight
with Percy from Gardening Hints ... he's always
asking me.

5 ERIC: What??   Parsnip Percy and his Gardening Column?
What a dope he is!!

6 HATTIE: He knows his job, anyway.   Everybody says he's
got green fingers.

7 ERIC: That's because he smokes celery.

9 HATTIE: Don't try to be funny.   I mean he knows all
about gardening!

10 ERIC: Gardening?   He thought a scarlet runner was
Emil Zatopek!   Now let's get on with the letters.

11 HATTIE: There's only one more left - and I think you'd
better read it yourself.

12 ERIC: Right.   "I am a beautiful young girl of eighteen,
and have had little experience of men.   My boy
friend never takes me out, but wants to sit in
the parlour every night and play ... and sometimes
he even .... (<u>giggles</u>)

13 HATTIE: What are you laughing at?

14 ERIC: Look at the way she spells "Canasta";

15 (<u>F/X Door opens</u>)

1 <u>ERNIE:</u>   Good morning Miss Lightbody.   Is the passion doctor finished?

2 HATTIE: From the look of him he can't have long to go.

3 <u>ERNIE:</u>   Come on Eric, the editor's sending us to Dartmoor.

4 ERIC: Why?   Has he been checking the Petty Cash?

5 <u>ERNIE:</u>   No!   We've got to interview an inventor at a village called Peacehaven.   I'll tell you the details in the train.

6 HATTIE: Why don't you go in Mr. Morecambe's car?

7 <u>ERNIE:</u>   You've got a car?   Well, why didn't we use it for that job last night?

8 ERIC: I never drive at night ... I can't see where I'm going.

9 <u>ERNIE:</u>   Why not?

10 ERIC: The wind keeps blowing the candles out!

11 <u>GRAMS:</u>   MUSIC LINK

                  (<u>FADE INTO</u>)

12   (<u>F/X</u> Street hoises.   Establish and lose)

13 ERIC: There's the car.   Isn't she a smasher?

14 <u>ERNIE:</u>   When did you make it?

15 ERIC: Make it??   I bought it ... and it was cheap too! I got it for a song.

16 <u>ERNIE:</u>   Even with your voice, you were still robbed. Anyway, it's too small.   Do you think two of us can get in there?

1 ERIC: Two!   There's room for four!! I've got a decoy
seat at the back.

2 ERNIE: You mean dicky seat. A decoy is something you
use to trap birds.

3 ERIC: I'm no mug!

4 ERNIE: Listen. You'd never get a girl to ride in this
car!

5 ERIC: Miss Lightbody's been in it a few times.

6 ERNIE: I know ... but you'd never get a girl in. Anyway
let's get going. How do you get her started.

7 ERIC: I give her a drop of gin.

8 ERNIE: The car?

9 ERIC: No ... Miss Lightbody!

10 ERNIE: Never mind her!! I'll use the starting handle.
Does she kick back?

11 ERIC: I don't know. I've never kicked Miss Lightbody.

12 ERNIE: I'm talking about the car!! Don't mention Miss
Lightbody again!!

13 ERIC: No Ernie ... (carries on following speech with
"Yes Ernie ... No Ernie"... etc.)

14 ERNIE: (still annoyed) Never again!! Understand??
Forget her!! We no longer know her!! I've
forgotten her name!!

15 ERIC: It's Angela.

1	ERNIE:	(Livid) Look!! Be quiet!! Forget it!! You silly, stupid, doddering nincompoop you!!!
2	ERIC:	You're cross aren't you? *with mr Rawn*
3	ERNIE:	(Quietly sarcastic) No. I'm not cross. No! No! I'm not annoyed at all.
4	ERIC:	Well what are you shouting at me for??
5	ERNIE:	How dare you raise your voice to me?
6	ERIC:	I'm sorry Ernie. I must have had a brainstorm.
7	ERNIE:	For that you need a brain!! Who taught you to read big words? I did!
8	ERIC:	Yes Ernie.
9	ERNIE:	Who got you a job as a reporter on the Morning Sun? I did!
10	ERIC:	Yes Ernie.
11	ERNIE:	Who taught you the facts of life? I did!!
12	ERIC:	No Ernie.
13	ERNIE:	Well who did?
14	ERIC:	*MISS LIGHTBODY* ~~That girl whose name I mustn't mention!~~
15	ERNIE:	Oh, what's the use!! Get in the car while I crank the starting handle.
16		(F/X starting handle cranked) (F/X Car starts up. Old noisy spluttering engine)
17	ERNIE:	*cue* (off) Right. Keep her going! I'll jump in!
18		(F/X Car door shuts) (F/X Car moves forward)

Onil.

1	ERIC:	We're off now. I say, this road slopes a lot doesn't it?
2	ERNIE:	You've got two wheels on the pavement, fathead. Pull over ... the other way! When did you learn to drive?
3	ERIC:	In the army - I was the general's chauffeur until I was court martialled for obeyingan order!
4	ERNIE:	Court martialled for obeying an order - what order?
5	ERIC:	The general said "Morecanbe, you'll drive me up the wall". So I did.
6		(F/X car passes them very fast, sounding horn)

On 12.

7	ERIC:	Look at that idiot!! Passing me on my left!
8	ERNIE:	I'm not surprised. You're driving on the right ~~hand side of the road~~!
9	ERIC:	Hey, look at that police van.
10	ERNIE:	Where?
11	ERIC:	That Black Maria in front! With the notice on the back?
12	ERNIE:	What does the notice say?
13	ERIC:	"Running in. Please pass."
14	GRAMS:	SHORT MUSIC LINK
		(FADE INTO)
15		(F/X Car running) *On E.*
16	ERIC:	Do you think I'm driving better now?

1 ERNIE: Yes.   The roads are beginning to turn when you do.

2 ERIC: Thanks ... Hey quick!   Take the wheel!   Here
comes another tree!!

3 ERNIE: I've had enough of this!   I'll drive from here.

4 ERIC: You can't drive from there - the steering wheel 's
over here.

5 ERNIE: Move over ... I'll slide under you!

6 ERIC: Isn't it a bit risky?

7 ERNIE: Nonsense!   Give me the wheel ... how get across
my knees ... don't lie across them, dope!

8 ERIC: ~~Oh.   You want me to sit on them.~~

9 ERNIE: ~~I don't want~~ ... Look out!   You're blocking my
view!

10 ERIC: I say.   Do you want to make a 'phone call?

11 ERNIE: Of course I don't.

12 ERIC: Well why are you heading strqight for that
telephone box?   Telephone box!!   We're going to
crash!   I'm sure we're going to crash!   I'm
certain we're going to crash!

13   (F/X crash)

                  (PAUSE)

14 ERIC: Mind you - I could be wrong!

15 GRAMS: MUSIC LINK

16 ERNIE: It was alucky thing we had the crash near a garage.

Extracts from Morecambe and Wise's 'Live' Touring Act of the 1970s

(Both Eric and Ernie walk on from stage right to loud applause from audience, both take a bow from the right hand side of the stage, and then one from the left. All this done to the theme of Bring Me Sunshine *played by the Johnny Wiltshire Sound, who are on stage behind them.)*

E.M.: Everybody. Ah, marvellous.

(Eric takes another bow.)

E.M.: Thank you.

(Ernie dances around.)

E.M.: Marvellous. *(To Ernie)* Have we got time for anymore?

E.W.: Yes, I think so.

E.M.: Oh, lovely.

(Eric straightens his glasses.)

E.W.: Lovely, that.

E.M.: Lovely.

E.W.: What a place.

E.W.: I've never worked in an aircraft hangar before.

E.M.: No.

(Eric says this with hands in his pockets looking around as if inspecting the place.)

E.M.: Are you gonna take off?

E.W.: I think so.

(Eric turns round to face the band behind him and puts his thumbs up.)

E.M.: And John, I think that was great.

Eric and Ernie leaving their dressing-room for a stage performance during one of their Morecambe and Wise Live tour dates of the seventies. Peeping through a crack is the executive producer of the touring show, and right-hand man of their agent Billy Marsh, Graham Stephenson.

E.W.: That was great.

(Johnny raises his hand in acknowledgement.)

E.M.: You did that superbly, you really did.

(Pause and Eric turns to audience with his hands still in his pockets.)

E.M.: Which is sad when you come to consider. However, you can't have everything in life.

E.W.: There's a terrible fracas going on at the side of the stage.

E.M.: Yeah … Eh?

E.W.: I said there's a terrible fracas going on out there.

(Eric turns his head away from Ernie and looks side stage.)

E.M.: Can he say fracas?

(Pause.)

E.M.: No. Fracas.

E.W.: Fracas.

(Eric nods his head at side of the stage.)

E.M.: No, but you were close.

E.M.: They're looking it up.

E.W.: Looking it up?

E.M.: But then again, they always did!

E.W.: They'll let us know later will they?

E.M.: They'll let you know later, yes.

(Eric touches his glasses with one hand, and drops it a second later.)

E.M.: It's a lovely place, isn't it?

E.W.: Yes, beautiful. Beautiful, isn't it?

E.M.: It's like a sauna bath with ants.

* * *

E.M.: *(Pointing towards audience)* Have we got a show for you tonight folks. Have we got a show for you tonight. *(Laughs nervously)* Hey, have we got a show for them tonight?

E.W.: Just.

(Eric slaps his hands together excitedly, then shakes them as if they hurt.)

E.M.: *(Pointing to audience and laughing)* I tell you what we have got. We've got a fella who's going to come on in a few minutes' time, he's really clever 'cos he swallows … oh yes, folks! … he swallows a four foot sword!

E.W.: What's clever about that?

E.M.: He's only three foot tall!

(As audience laugh, Eric and Ernie both talk under their breath to each other for a second.)

E.M.: He's back there at the moment like that. *(Bends his leg at funny angle and leans to one side)* It's agony for him! He doesn't know where to put his hat.

(Eric grabs Ernie's arm.)

E.M.: *(Quietly)* But he has found a place, I'm told.

E.M.: My god, it's all going on … you're working well, Ern.

(Ernie stands there, arms crossed.)

E.M.: You're working well … you can't see the join. *(Points to Ernie's hair)* that's one of the best you've ever had that. It's a beauty!

(Ernie proudly tapping his hair as Eric says this.)

E.M: It arrived this morning all the way from Axminster … on its own. You should have seen it climbing up those steps!

(Eric uses his hand to help visualise the image.)

E.M.: Like the beast with five fingers. Aaaahhghgh!!!!!

E.W.: I've shampooed it.

E.M.: Eh?

E.W.: I've just shampooed it.

E.M.: With what?

(Laugh from Ernie and then from Eric.)

E.W.: *(Suddenly serious)* You're using the wrong approach.

E.M.: Who is?

E.W.: You is.

E.M.: Oh! Am I?

E.W.: Yes. You've got to get friendly with the audience.

E.M.: Oh yes, I suppose you have. I'm not a complete fool, you know.

E.W.: Why, what part's missing?

E.M.: We allow him one … and that was it. It's uphill from now on.

E.W.: You do it by facing them, making a funny remark about someone in the audience, then they're on your side.

(Eric slaps Ernie's chest and leaves his hand there for a few seconds. He then puts his arm around Ernie and with the other hand slaps Ernie's face repeatedly.)

* * *

E.M.: Make fun about them, laugh about them and everybody does. Everybody laughs. *(Eric laughs aloud)* There's some funny people about, ain't there? Everyone in the front row is saying to themselves, 'I hope to God they don't pick on me'.

E.W.: It's true!

E.M.: You can see it in their eyes, they'll all going …

(Eric imitates someone desperately trying to mind their own business and not be noticed.)

E.M.: However, I've got one.

E.W.: Haven't we all?

E.M.: You dirty little devil.

E.W.: I …

E.M.: Hello lady!

E.W.: Hello lady!

E.M.: By golly, aren't you fat!

E.W.: *(Putting his hands on his side and walking around in disbelief)* No!!!

E.M.: What a fat woman you are.

E.W.: Don't say that.

E.M.: Did you come on a lorry? How did you get in? … More to the point, how're you gonna get out?

E.W.: I'm sorry madam, he's just pulling your leg.

E.M.: I couldn't even lift it! Have you seen it? It's enormous, Ern! There's a big, enormous woman over there. *(Takes glasses off, worriedly)* It's a fella!

*   *   *

E.W.: I'm perspiring freely here.

E.M.: *(Facing the audience)* It's the heat you know, the lights and everything.

E.W.: Yes. *(Pause)* The difference between you and I is I perspire and you sweat.

E.M.: I suppose so, yes. *(Pause)* I wish I had the nerve to do that.

E.W.: The nerve to do what?

E.M.: Well … in public like that.

E.W.: You've got a handkerchief in your top pocket.

E.M.: *(In a low voice)* It's me shirt!

E.W.: It's your shirt? A shirt in your top pocket?

E.M.: Yes, yes.

E.W.: You've come all the way to the Fairfield's Hall, Croydon – this classy joint – and you had the … You're making us look like a cheap music hall act.

E.M.: We *are* a cheap music hall act, whaddya mean?

E.W.: *They* don't know.

E.M.: *(Genuinely laughing)* I'm sure they do! *(Ernie laughs too. Then he pulls on Eric's 'handkerchief' and Eric's left leg rises)* Don't do that. It's my shirt! *(Ernie does it again.)*

E.W.: *(Turning away from Eric and looking searchingly out into the audience)* I'd like to give a warm welcome to my fan club here tonight.

E.M.: Oh, lovely. Where's he sat?

E.W.: *(Pointing)* Just over there.

E.M.: *(Giving a small wave)* Hello sir, nice to see you again. *(To Ernie)* Follows you everywhere doesn't he?

E.W.: All the way from Carlisle.

E.M.: On a handcart. Marvellous. Fabulous that. *(Nods his head and then adjusts his glasses.)*

E.W.: Nice to see you again, Rodney.

E.M.: Who is it this time?

E.W.: Rodney.

E.M.: What happened to Esmey? *(Pause)* Not a lot, I'm told. *(Ernie laughs at this.)*

E.W.: *(Suddenly)* You don't think I get fan mail, do you?

E.M.: *(Looking shocked and grabbing Ernie's arm)* Good Lord, no!

E.W.: *(Impersonating American film star James Cagney)* Well, that's where you're wrong, you dirty rat, you!

E.M.: John Wayne?

E.W.: No … *(Moves closer to Eric)* You dirty rat!

E.M.: You're on me foot!

E.W.: Freddie Starr! *(Pause)* I've got a fan letter here.

E.M.: That's a relief.

(Ernie produces a letter from his pocket.)

E.W.: I'd better read it. I'm getting nowhere with my…

E.M.: Impressions.

E.W.: Impressions.

E.M.: Your Freddie Starr.

E.W.: My Freddie Starr. It says – it's so small I can't see it. Can I borrow your glasses?

E.M.: Is that all it says? You see, I can't class that as fan mail: 'Dear Mr Wise, can I borrow your glasses,' signed a well-wisher. I can't…

E.W.: No, no. Can I borrow your glasses so I can read this fan letter to the gathered assembly?

E.M.: I didn't realise that. Of course you may.

(Eric hands his glasses to Ernie, but not where he is standing. Ernie sighs, takes them and puts them on. Ernie looks at Eric and Eric laughs loudly at him.)

E.W.: I'll read this fan mail.

E.M.: Yes, do that.

E.W.: *(Reading)* 'Dear Morecambe and Wise, I like you very much, but my favourite is the one with the glasses.'

E.M.: Thank you, thank you *(then expression changes as he remembers Ernie has his glasses).*

E.W.: I'm the favourite.

E.M.: *(Snatching his glasses back from Ernie)* I get fan mail too, matey. You don't think so, do you?

E.W.: No, I don't.

E.M.: Well, I do.

E.W.: Not as good as me.

E.M.: Better than your fan mail, matey *(feeling jacket)* … if I've got the right jacket on! If I haven't then there could be a minute's silence! *(Both men suddenly face the audience perfectly still and silent. Then Eric rechecks his pockets and produces a piece of paper.)* Wanna hear this?

E.W.: Yes, please.

E.M.: *(Rustles paper in microphone. Clears his throat.)* Dear Mr Morecambe, you can't sing, you can't dance, you're not funny. *(Ernie smiles smugly.)* P.S. Get rid of your partner, he's dragging you down!

E.W.: It doesn't say that.

E.M.: Oh yes it does.

E.W.: We've had another special request.

E.M.: What?

E.W.: You can stay!

E.M.: *(Laughing)* Oh! Another gem hit the dust.

E.W.: I'm going to sing a little song.

E.M.: What?

E.W.: It goes something like this…

* * *

E.M.: *(To audience)* Any questions you want to ask us? Anything at all? We don't mind. Anything? *(Nervous laughter from audience, clearly not expecting this.)*

E.M.: Eh?

Voice from audience: Who's going to win the cup?

E.M.: It won't be Crystal Palace, I can promise you that! Not doing too bad, Luton. Doing very well Luton are at the moment. We play

Middlesbrough next week. If we beat Middlesbrough at Middlesbrough that's four points to us that, because we cheat! Very good, that. Any other questions?

(Indistinct voice from audience.)

E.M.: Pardon? When are we coming back? We'll be here tomorrow! Pardon? The 'Two Old Men Sitting in Deckchairs' joke? Well, there were two old men sitting in deckchairs and one old man says, 'It's nice out' and the other says, 'Yes it is, I think I'll take mine out!' *(Pause till laughter subsides)* Any other questions? Any at all?

E.M.: I've gotta stop doing that you know. *(Playing with his hands in his pockets)* No I mustn't, it's becoming a habit that. It's getting to the point where it's fun.

E.W.: Anything else?

E.M.: Pardon?

E.W.: Anything else?

E.M.: Anything else?

E.W.: Sex life?

E.M.: You want to know about his sex life?

('Yes!' chorused back from the audience.)

E.M.: I thought you would. I thought you would, you'll have to buy the book, it's called *Eric and Ern* and it's all about his sex life.

E.W.: Yes, yes.

E.M.: One chapter, 24 blank pages, and a full stop at the end.

*   *   *

(Question suddenly from the audience.)

E.M.: Pardon, love?

Voice from audience: Are you signing autographs later?

E.M. + E.W.: Yes, yes.

E.M.: We'll do it now if you've got a long arm. *(Long pause while laughter subsides)* You see this is a special year for Ern and I, you see, because we are celebrating er, de, lum, er…

E.W.: Thirty-four years together.

E.M.: Thirty-four years together, ever since we were kids, it's true that.

(More prolonged applause) Marvellous, really. *(Turning to Ernie)* If we ever split, you'd never forget me would you? Ha, ha, ha, look at me when I'm talking to you. If we split you'd never forget me would you? Hey!

E.W.: After thirty-four years together.

E.M.: What?

E.W.: Kids together.

E.M.: We haven't, have we?

(Eric laughs.)

E.W.: No. I'll never forget you *(gives Eric friendly punch on the arm. Eric grabs his arm as if it to hurt him)*. No! I'll never forget you. Never!

E.M.: Knock-knock.

E.W.: Who's there?

E.M.: You see what I mean, you've forgotten me already, haven't you!

(Both leave stage to the band playing Bring Me Sunshine, *both walk back on, bow and walk off. Eric goes and shakes Johnny Wiltshire's hand then waves to audience and exits. Both return to continued applause.)*

E.W.: *(Having removed jacket and undone his shirt)* Honestly, we were coming back.

E.M.: No, it's been marvellous. Do me a favour, look at that *(points to Ernie's chest hair)*. Now, were you born or trapped? *(Back to audience)* It's been lovely – no, you've been a marvellous audience, but we can't stay any longer purely because we've got a large queue of people round for the next house – and we've run out of jokes. We'll take one more question – anything at all.

(Murmur from audience.)

E.M.: 'Fracas'! We never found out. It's one of those that we're not bothered about. *(To side of stage)* What's 'fracas'? Good Lord, he's fainted. *(Both laugh)* He's just found out! *(To audience)* What was that about the hairy legs? Just a quick flash, Ern *(Ernie pulls up trouser leg to cheers and applause. Eric puts his glasses on Ernie's leg, giving the impression of a hairy face)*.

E.M.: Thanks folks, that's all!

(Both exit side stage for the last time to theme of Bring Me Sunshine, *played by the band.)*

Ends...

In Eric's words
Morecambe on Fishing

People always ask me if Ernie really does wear a wig. I'm sworn to secrecy, but let's just say that he keeps Axminster Carpets in business. Without him, they'd be on the floor.

Much of my father's childhood, as we have seen, was coloured by days spent fishing, mostly with his dad.

In the room which was once his office and was also the subject of an unusual documentary for Channel 4 a few years ago, I found, among his myriad possessions, a handful of pages on his great passion for fishing. These were destined for a book he wrote about fishing in 1983 and which was published posthumously the following year.

What grabbed me about the first section, entitled 'The Anti-Fishermen', was the frankness with which he wrote. His views are balanced, yet I still came away from reading it feeling a little uncomfortable that a gentle and loving comedian, who worked quite hard at avoiding controversial topics, could suddenly let himself go. A part of me is also very proud that he did: it would be so easy for him to have ignored the issue in such a book and just gone for easy laughs. Mind you, I think the line about the African elephant is more controversial now than it was back then.

Eric typed the following material on his own office typewriter some six months before his sudden death in May 1984.

The Anti-Fishermen

In recent months there have been fresh eruptions from the hunt saboteurs, who threaten to move in on our sport and disrupt it. The saboteurs would have you believe that fishing is cruel and should be completely banned. By fishing they mean freshwater fishing in rivers, lakes and reservoirs. Sea fishing, for some odd reason, is always left out of their arguments.

Strangely enough I have some sympathy for some of the ideas put forward by the anti-hunting lobby. At the same time, I have a strong feeling that if any hunt saboteurs came barging in on the stretch where I fish, then the shotguns would be out and the saboteurs could well be threatened with a dose of pellets in the pants. And I wouldn't mind that at all.

If I seem to be facing both ways at once in this controversy, let me quickly say that I am fundamentally on the side of the people who enjoy their country sports and wish to continue doing so. Where I have reservations, increasingly as I grow older, is in the quantity of animals killed and in some of the methods applied.

In fishing, I wish there could be almost no killing, but until someone invents a rubber hook I can't see that happening. I don't personally like live-baiting, the process whereby a live fish – a Dace, say, or a Roach or Rudd – is impaled on a hook, or Jardine snap-tackle, and set as bait to lure a bigger fish such as a Pike. Fewer people go in for live-baiting nowadays than used to in Victorian times, but it is still an accepted method in the fishing community. Dead-baiting I do not mind so much. If the fish is already dead, then the question of its feeling pain does not arise. But, as I said in a previous

Eric caught in a lovely moment — genuinely relaxed, his mind on bird-watching and fishing. These were the times when he was at his most content.

chapter, it is the quality of the individual catch that really matters, not how many fish end up in your keep-net or freezer-bags. Some fishermen are a little bit inclined to see their sport too much in terms of match-angling, of collecting fish by the bagful, and not enough in terms of hunting for the best single adversary to be found in a particular stretch of water.

What the anti-fishing lobby does not seem to understand, often because its members have no day-to-day contact with the countryside, is that it is necessary to cull certain species of wildlife if we are to preserve the present balance in nature. No one could manage a dairy farm that has more foxes than cows, and no one wants a river that is so full of fish you could walk across it on their backs; it's no good for the fish, quite apart from anything else.

In Africa, too, it may seem sad that men have to go out and shoot

*Eric's favourite
pastime. About to
hit the riverbank
with his fellow-
fisherman and
family friend, Guy
Hammersley.*

such magnificent creatures as the elephants, and yet it has been proved time and time again that the well-run game reserve, with its organised programme of culling, is by far the best means of preserving a good balance in nature. Take away the game reserve, and what you get is the terrible greed and savagery of poachers, and the region loses many more elephants than it would have done, or needs to do, given a properly organised system.

Fishing in Britain is well organised. It has to be. About three million people go fishing each year and it is essential that the places they go to are properly controlled. The National Federation of Anglers plays a big part in this, seeing that competitions are run according to a fixed set of rules and that people enjoy their sport in a sensible, restrained way. On privately owned waters, the bailiffs keep out the poachers – or try to – and the number of fishermen per stretch of

water is carefully limited. On that basis, no saboteur or anyone else could really claim that fishing is the unthinking slaughter it is sometimes made out to be.

His next chapter is more reflective than combative, yet no less fascinating. I'd never taken time out to read his thoughts on fishing before, and the man writing about his favourite pastime is a long way from the comic father I remember so vividly.

Wherever Next?

Although we have our seasons for coarse and game fishing, no one has told the fish. As a result, they will accept our baits, lures and flies just about all the year round. The seasons are part of a system of man-made rules, and we stick to them because it makes sense to respect the breeding patterns of the fish and not to overwork the waters they live in. Nevertheless, you can find variations.

Trout fishing on the Test is from May to September, but on the local reservoirs near me they start around the beginning of March. Finding a place to fish is really a bit like getting a drink in a pub or hotel. If you try hard enough, and are prepared to travel around a bit – like to the old Covent Garden market in the early hours of the morning – you can always get one. With trout, too, there's always somewhere open. You may have to go abroad, but that is usually no hardship. Not to me, it isn't, although I must say I haven't yet been abroad on an out-and-out fishing holiday. Blame it on the wife, if you like, but on a family holiday we always prefer to go around together and do the same things. Joan isn't interested in fishing, and my son (Steven) prefers coarse fishing, so we aren't exactly three minds with but a single thought. Blame it on work as well. I have had one or two nice offers of trips abroad but couldn't go because I had to work for some or all of the period of the holiday.

Before the 1982 World Cup, I was invited to go to Spain and do a commentary for New Zealand Radio on the New Zealand team. That would give me two weeks in Spain – they didn't expect to last more than three games – and then we hit the real perk. This was to fly, with my wife, to New Zealand for six weeks of trout fishing in the big lakes they have there. I couldn't do it for the simple reason that I was working. It's funny that, but it always seems to happen. On the other hand, I've had plenty of times when I've wanted to work and couldn't get a job. There's no justice ...

The really big trips for the holiday fisherman take him nowadays to places like Iceland and Alaska. Just the sort of country you've always wanted to visit? Probably not, if you aren't a fisherman. If you are, and money is little or no object, then a magnificent holiday awaits.

I have several friends whose addiction for hanging about near the Arctic Circle for a few weeks each year is getting serious. They fish for salmon, which are not in short supply over there. The only trouble with that is what do you do at the end of your holiday with twenty-five salmon? In fact you could even make friends with people you didn't want to be friends with. There is just one snag. What about the transport; the excess baggage? Work out, if you can, how much excess you would have to pay on twenty-five salmon weighing twenty pounds (9kg) each, given a free allowance, assuming you travel First Class (which you would) of sixty-six pounds (30kg) with unlimited excess (which you wouldn't get) charged at a rate to be agreed with the airline. Not easy. The upshot is, my friends come home with about four fish each, which they have had smoked to get their weight down as far as possible.

Now, they will forgive me, I hope, but I don't altogether see the point of that. It may sound a bit eccentric but if I had caught twenty-five salmon in Alaska, I'd want to bring the whole lot home. It may not be easy, but that is what I would want to do. When I got them back here, I wouldn't necessarily give them away – not all of them. I expect I would invest in an enormous freezer and stick them in there while I thought about it for a few weeks. After all, if I could afford a medium-sized fortune to go and catch them in Alaska, I could certainly afford an enormous freezer to house them in back home. Any offers?

Two Old Men in Deckchairs

I was at Luton Football Club last Saturday. We were playing Arsenal. It was nice to meet the directors of their board. Nice club, Arsenal. Well, the first four letters are right.

I started following Chelsea FC when I was twelve. My parents bought me their team strip – that wonderful all-blue shirt and shorts that somehow even managed to look blue on black and white TV – and I was hooked. Then Eric became involved with Luton Town FC and for the next fourteen years Chelsea came a poor second in my football affiliations. But in 1985, when Chelsea were struggling more than Luton Town, I ended up moving to that part of west London. Those days were the dizzy heights when fixtures with Watford or Grimsby on a wet Wednesday evening meant acquiring a ticket wasn't exactly a challenge or a great expense. Not like it is now, as Chelsea have become Chelski under owner Roman Abramovich.

I've always kept an eye out for Luton, and was sorry to see them freefall and eventually leave the Football League for the first time in their history. I recall the days when they were sixth from top in the Premier League (then Division One) and beating sides like Manchester United and Arsenal. As Luton slip, Morecambe FC rise and for the first time in their history they have entered the Football League. What a thrill it would have given my father, who used to watch 'half the game', as he put it, from his bedroom window as one of the stands at the ground shielded his view and meant he could only see half the pitch.

I returned to the town last year after being invited to see a match between Luton and Coventry. People at the club are always so kind, and everyone seems to have a memory of Eric from the days when he was a director there.

The man in charge of car parking was quick to tell me of the time someone threw a coin on the pitch and hit the referee. 'It cut him quite badly, and he had to go off for a minute. After the match, Eric came straight down from the directors' box to see him. "Are you all right?" he asked. "Yes, fine, Eric," he replied. "Are you sure you don't want to go for further medical checks?" said Eric. "No, really, I'm OK," said the ref. "Oh, good," said Eric. "Then can I have my coin back?"'

There's an often repeated piece of radio commentary where Eric is being interviewed during the middle of a Luton match. Everything is how one would expect when someone is being interviewed on radio, then Luton score and suddenly one gets a genuine insight into Eric's boy-like love of 'the beautiful game'

p. 225 Eric photographed at home and looking very relaxed.

and the club he supports. Whenever it crops up it makes me smile, because this is my father as I knew him, not Eric Morecambe the comedian, being interviewed. It's the closest you will ever get to touching the real human being.

Eric was also a big cricket fan. In his final years he claimed he took more pleasure from an afternoon at Lord's watching England bat – or, to put it Rory Bremner's way, 'Listening to the sound of leather on stump!' – than sitting in the directors' box at Luton watching another struggle on the artificial turf they were then playing on.

My father's involvement with the charitable organization the Lord's Taverners was based on his love of cricket. The following piece of writing is something I found in his desk a while back. Whether it was ever published in the Taverners' magazine or not, I cannot say, but it makes interesting reading and shows as much of Eric the man as it does of Eric the comedian.

But first a little background to the content of the piece: in the early sixties, when Morecambe and Wise were suddenly making it big for Lew Grade's ATV, it became a running gag for a while to end each show with Eric telling a supposedly risky joke but unable to complete it because Ernie interrupts to say that they've run out of time. The joke always began, 'There were two old men sat in deckchairs, and one old man says to the other, "It's nice out," and the other old man says … ' At this point Ernie would interrupt, explaining either that time had run out or it was too rude to say on television. As far as I know, they never did complete the joke, though in the seventies, when doing their UK 'Live' tour, they would often get asked what the whole gag was during a Q&A at the end of each performance. And they would tell it in full. It was short and simple. 'There were two old men sat in deckchairs, and one old man says to the other, "It's nice out," and the other old man says, "Yes, it is; I think I'll take mine out!"'

Was this on his mind, I wonder, when he wrote the article I would find in his desk entitled *Two Old Men in Deckchairs*? Beneath the title it says 'By an Ex President', confirmation that this was written for the Lord's Taverners charity, of which Eric was President for three consecutive years. It is a charity that mostly works for young deprived people through sport, fundamentally cricket. Also the material itself bears out that this is the charity in question, especially as Eric himself makes an appearance in the little tale. The story also refers to a

Eric in conversation with actor John Alderton. The photo was taken at the Bear Inn Woodstock, Oxfordshire after a Lord's Taverners' charity cricket day in the grounds of Bleinhem Palace. Eric and Alderton met several times through Taverners' functions, and worked together in one of Charles Wallace's Betjeman films.

certain well-known radio and television presenter who was a friend of Eric and a fellow Taverner.

Two Old Men in Deckchairs

There were two old men sat in deckchairs. One old man was the son – he was sixty – the other old man was the father – he was eighty-six.

'Are you comfortable, father?' the son asked.

'What? Eh?' the father asked.

'Are you comfortable?' the son repeated.

'I can't hear you: speak up!' the father shouted.

The son knew why the father couldn't hear him, so he leaned over and turned up his deaf aid a shade (a portable one, about the size of Wisden's 120th edition). The father looked down on what the son was doing and hit him.

'Don't you dare turn that thing off so you can't hear me!' The son smiled at one or two people around him, as if to say 'Don't worry, this always happens' then put a cushion at the back of his father.

'Should be a nice day for the game,' remarked the son. The father looked about wondering who it was who'd spoken. It was half a minute before he realized it was the son.

'Put my cushion at the back of this deckchair, there's a good boy,' said the father. The younger of the two old men knew that his father was playing silly sods with him for the benefit of the people around. But the son was up to his father's tricks.

'Pardon?' he said to his father.

'What?' the father said to his son.

'Alright, what?' said the son to his father. The father then realized that the son had realized that he was playing silly sods, so he went quiet.

'Would you like to see the programme, father?' The father ignored the last comment completely. The people around them giggled behind backs of hands. The father looked at the people and giggled too.

'He's my son, you know!' He said this to all and sundry putting his hand up to his head and, pointing one finger to his temple, made a whirring motion which suggested his son had lost his marbles. Then, with his watery grey eyes dripping acid, looked up at his son and laughed. The son didn't look back because he already knew what was going on. The father was in the mood for entertaining the crowd at his son's expense. 'I come here every year,' he said to a young, big-breasted woman of about fifty-five. (Well, she was young to him.) 'Have you been here before?' the old man asked. The young big-breasted woman of about fifty-five smiled a smile reserved for old men, and in a very loud voice (as all old men are deaf) shouted, 'No!' straight into his deaf aid. The old man's eyes spun around while he shakily turned down the volume control.

The son noticed what the old man had done and while the older man's eyes were still swivelling in their sockets quickly turned the aid up again. The people around giggled, so the unknowing old man giggled, too.

'It's a nice day for cricket,' said the son.

'Where's the Gents?' asked the father loud enough for all to hear. The crowd dutifully giggled again.

'You're wearing it!' the son said. His father went quiet for the next few minutes.

In the distance you could see the back of Blenheim Palace. It's an enormous building; almost as big as Northampton. The deckchairs, ringed around the cricket pitch, were filling up nicely. To the left of where the two old men in deckchairs were sat two men dressed in their cricket whites emerged from a wooden dressing room. They walked slowly towards the crease to toss a coin.

'Which is Oxford University?' asked the old man.

'The one in white!' teased the son.

'They're both in white!'

'No, father,' said the son. 'The one from Oxford is in white.' He pointed to the two captains. 'The other one used to be white.'

The old man turned to the big-breasted woman of about fifty-five and said, 'I used to know Pelham Warner as a boy.' He blinked his damp eyes at her.

'That's nice,' she replied loudly. 'Was he a nice boy?' Everybody laughed, and the old man looked uncertain as to what they were laughing at, so joined in with them.

'Who won the toss?' the son asked his father.

'The banking people are going to field,' came his reply.

'What banking people?'

'The Lloyds Taverners!' said the father.

Everyone giggled even more, except the young big-breasted woman of about fifty-five. She was talking to her husband, asking if he'd heard of Pelham Warner. Her husband said he was sure it was somewhere near the end of the Northern line.

A ragged line of Lord's Taverners walked to the middle of the playing area, and stood motionless a moment like scattered washing hung out to dry. Four ex-England players threw the ball at each other while the stars chatted to each other. The ex-England players threw the ball about like it was a magnet and their hands made of metal; under arm, over arm, a flick with the wrist, out of the back of the hand. It was great to watch. One of them threw the ball to a star who caught it very well, but had to go off for attention to a badly bruised hand. Two ambulance men, both dressed like Benny Hill, dashed around the enclosure where the star was enclosed watching his guitar fingering hand throbbing and turning from a bright red to a pale blue.

'That'll be stiff in the mornin',' said the older Benny Hill.

'It's bloody stiff now,' said the guitar playing star. 'Will I be able to play?'

'Should be all right, but don't field too close to the bat.'

'I mean, will I be able to play the guitar?'

'Oh!' said the older Benny Hill.

'I've got a gig tonight.'

'Oh! Well,' said the older Benny Hill scratching his head, 'you'll never be able to drive one of them things tonight.'

'Ice!' exclaimed the, until now, silent younger Benny Hill. 'Ice's what that wants!'

'OK, well can you find me some ice?' said the guitar playing star trying to stifle his anxiety.

The younger Benny Hill turned to the older Benny Hill. 'Got any ice, George?'

'No,' replied the older Benny Hill.

The younger Benny Hill turned to the injured guitar playing star.

'No we ain't. Sorry 'bout that.'

p.231 Eric and Ernie advertising Tenants' beer.

'You see, sir,' said the older Benny Hill through an expression that suggested latent wisdom, 'we don't carry ice packs with us as they would melt!'

'Yes, that's what ice does,' agreed the younger Benny Hill with a brief nod.

'There's a bar over there,' pointed the injured guitar playing star with his good hand. 'Can you ask them for some, please? Tell them it's an emergency.'

The Taverners' team were now standing in a group waiting to have their photo taken for the local paper. In their midst stood an ageing ex-President with pads on the wrong way up and pretending to hit a ball with the handle of the bat. He wore an old England cap with the peak facing the wrong way, and his glasses askew so they pointed to one side. The photographer called out, 'Look this way!' and every-body looked his way. 'Now, can you think of something else funny to do?' he asked, and the ex-President picked up one of the stumps and placed it in his mouth like a cigar. One of the other stars picked up another stump and made to stab it in to the heart of the ex-President, which if done for real would have made him a very ex ex-President!

'Great!' said the photographer, and he and the ex-President wad-dled off the pitch together. As they walked, the photographer asked the ex-President if he wouldn't mind dressing in women's clothes and doing something funny with two cricket balls and a stump. Mean-while, the players moved into their allotted positions in the outfield. One or two are doing stretches as way of warm up exercises. The stars stand and rub their hands together as if they've heard they're going to be paid. The umpire walks out with a shooting stick and plants it in the ground and sits on it. As the game progresses it seems possible the shooting stick is sinking further and further into the ground.

'The game's started,' said the old man's old son.

'I can't see what's going on for that fella there!' grumbled the father. He pointed to a cricketer parked in front of the old man's deckchair. The star cricketer turned around and smiled and said, through a soft Irish brogue and immaculately polished teeth, 'You ought to be thankful: I have to watch it!' And with this, he moves like a panther – albeit a very old and rather tired panther – out of the old man's view.

'Cheeky sod!' said the old man to his son.

'Shh! Father. That's Terry Wogan.'

'Who?'

'Terry Wogan, father.'

'Oh, I remember him. Saw him just before the war at the pier theatre, Yarmouth. Yes, Wogan and MacShane. He used to dress up as an old woman. That's it – he was Old Mother Riley.'

Mr Wogan heard nothing of this as he fell down to a ball at the same time turning a similar colour in his attempt to prevent a boundary. By the time he'd managed to throw the ball back to the approximately correct vicinity, the two Oxford batsmen had run Five!

The tannoy boomed out the score and followed through with a 'Thaaaank yoooouu, Mister Woooogannnn.'

Terry, as everyone called him, waved a jovial arm.

'Good shot!' called the old man's son as the Oxford batsman facing hit a mighty drive. Wogan turned and gave him a quizzical stare.

'Yarmouth, 1938!' said the old man catching Mister Wogan's eye.

Mister Wogan smiled the smile that has captivated at least a dozen TV viewers down the years, cupped his hands around his mouth and shouted, 'Yes, and I waited for you, but you didn't show up!'

The old man, who hadn't heard a word, turned to his old son and said, 'You see, I was right.'

The over ended and Mister Wogan waved to the crowd who cheered everything he did, as he moved off to another field placement.

The tannoy blared out the fact that the Polaroid Enclosure was now ready, and some of the stars of the greatest magnitude were waiting to have their pictures taken with the public for only one pound.

'What's the score?' the old man asked his son.

'Oxford are one hundred and ten for three.'

'They'll walk it. That Lloyds Taverners lot won't get anywhere near that score.'

'LORD'S Taverners,' corrected his son. 'And they've got some pretty good players, Dad.'

'Then where are they hiding 'em? Good God, that Old Mother Riley fella's over ninety.'

'Terry Wogan, father.'

'Yes – saw him back in 1938 … '

'Terry Wogan's with Jimmy Young.'

'In those days he was Kitty MacShane.'

The tannoy told everyone that actor Patrick Mower was in the Polaroid Enclosure and waiting for photos to be taken with the public.

'Who did he say was there?' asked the old man.

'Patrick Mower.'

'Oh yes, I like him. The Sky at Night. Good TV, that.'

'I wouldn't mind having a picture taken with him,' said the big-breasted woman of about fifty-five. Her husband looked at her for about the first time in two weeks.

The game ambled on.

The Duke and Duchess wandered around and waved to everyone. The guitar playing star left the ground because he couldn't get any ice for his swollen hand. He went home in his chauffeur driven Bugatti to his mum in North Acton.

The younger old man looked to his left and saw something that made him turn to his father and whisper into his deaf aid. The old man looked up as quickly as any old man could, and they both closed their eyes as two ex-England players and two stars (one female) walked by them carrying a large sheet full of notes to go to the charity.

The game was going well. Tea was taken. The other side were put in. The game ended with the Taverners winning by one run. It rained. The sun came out. The wind blew. It froze hard. It thundered. Fog came down. The sun came out again. It was a perfect English summer's day. Nearly everyone had drifted away except for the two old men sat in deckchairs.

'Well, father. Did you enjoy that?' asked the son.

'Bloody awful!'

'Yes, I'm looking forward to next year, too.'

'And me, but I won't be coming here if Old Mother Riley's playing!'

My Lords and Gentlemen

I try not to think what I'd do if he [Ernie] wasn't around. I expect I'd take six months off, then try another show with another partner, another straight man. No, not exactly a straight man, because Ernie's not a straight man: like Tony Hancock had Sid James, someone like that … it wouldn't be another double act: it wouldn't be The Eric Morecambe–Charlie Smith Show. But I need a partner; on my own I just prattle on. Ernie senses this; he knows when I'm going off and he brings me down to earth with exactly the right line, and that's marvellous.

The Lord's Taverners took up much of my father's time, particularly during his three-year reign as President during the late seventies.

When I found a segment of one of the many speeches he made during his life, I assumed – erroneously as it transpires – that it was one of his addresses to his fellow Taverners at a charity dinner held at the Café Royal in London. But the

Eric signing autographs at the annual Lord's Taverners charity cricket match at Blenheim Palace, Oxfordshire.

content suggested otherwise, and it quickly became apparent that it was made to a male gathering of governors and staff of my own former school, Aldenham. I never knew a thing about this event until I discovered the following:

MY LORDS AND GENTLEMEN. I think that takes in most of you. Now I suppose you are all sat there wondering why I've sent for you. The answer is simple: It's to say thank-you on behalf of the guests – who-ever he is – for a most delightful evening – so it says here!

You are all probably saying to yourselves, 'I thought he was taller than that?' Well, I'm not. 'If he's only that tall his partner must be small.' As a matter of fact, he is small. So small, he is here tonight and we haven't found him yet.

When I was first invited to reply on behalf of the guests, I said, 'What shall I talk about?' They said, 'About three minutes!'

Now it's very difficult for me to stand here and talk about a subject I know very little about — Education. Because the school I went to was different: you had to be sent there by a Judge!

Of course, the secret of a good speech is to be sincere — you must be sincere, whether you mean it or not.

I'm told that if I make a good speech I can return next year. I'm also told that if I make a VERY good speech I can return next year and won't have to eat the meal.

Not that there is anything wrong with the food or the service at the Café Royal.

Eric and Joan on their terrace above the garden pond of their Harpenden home. Eric is wearing his Lord's Taverners country tie.

As always, it's first class. You might have happened to notice there are three waiters for each person. Simple, really. One gives you the bill, the other two are there to revive you!

There was a little trouble here a few weeks back. The waiters went on strike for three days. But they had to give it up as nobody noticed the difference.

And please, I beg you, don't be disparaging about the coffee. You may be old and weak yourself some day.

The committee, who had the problem of organising this evening for you, wanted to do something a little different. At a given point, a great big six foot cake was to be wheeled into the room, and a naked girl was going to pop out. But when we took the cake out the oven this afternoon she didn't look too good, so we scrubbed around the idea.

I have two children. One goes to Aldenham, but the other one has fortunately kept on the straight and narrow. My son tells me that the school was founded in the year 1597, in the reign of Glenda Jackson. And according to him they still have the same cooks!

It's a pity, of course, that none of the original buildings exist anymore. The earliest building there dates from 1825 — which as you all

Eric at a book signing session for Mr Lonely, *his novel about a stand-up comedian.*

know is 25 past 6. The New Chapel was 1937, which is almost 20 to 8. If you work that out, it took them 2 hours and fifteen minutes to build the chapel.

The beauty of a school like Aldenham, apart from Mrs Wallace-Hadrill [a housemaster's wife] is that nowadays, with education being the way it is, your son has the opportunity of growing up and becoming Prime Minister — which is one of the chances he has to take.

Everyone has the same opportunity as the next person. All men are created equal. The man who said that was a fool. The man who said all men are created equal has never been in a footballers' dressing-room.

I asked my son if he'd like to go into politics. I wouldn't object — he has a great sense of humour! I myself don't belong to any organised party — I vote Liberal! But you take the state of the country today. People are complaining there aren't enough houses. I say Rubbish! That's just a vicious rumour started by people with nowhere to live.

My brother-in-law built his own five bedroomed bungalow last year, very close to London, for £1,800. He found the plot himself, drew up the plans himself and economised by stealing the bricks!

The Common Market is proving a problem. We have our own customs in England – we drink our wine out of glasses. In France they drink their wine out of doors. It's not nice, that. And what about their driving? Over there they all drive on the right hand side of the road. Over here only the women do that.

Does the government know that there are more TV sets in this country than bathrooms? Which proves there are a lot of dirty people watching the Morecambe and Wise Show.

However, I digress. Let's get back to Aldenham and education. A recent survey shows that out of 974 school teachers in this country, 201 proved conclusively that they were!

I remember my wife saying – we were talking that day – she said what a marvellous job teachers do – and I agree, because the human

One of my personal favourites. Author's first wedding, 11 October 1980. Eric's nephew Paul Bartlett has said something which has certainly tickled his uncle.

239

brain is a most wonderful piece of mechanism. It starts functioning the moment you wake up in the morning, and doesn't stop until you get to the office. I feel that teachers, and in particular headmasters, have a tremendous responsibility. My old headmaster, when I left school, said to me – 'Bartholomew, I'm sorry to see you go. You've been like a son to me: Insolent, surly and unappreciative.'

But when I was at school we didn't have the facilities of today. Just take the Aldenham school library alone. My son brings home some fantastic books. I've read some and they've taught me a thing or to.

There was this one book – I forget the title but it was a sad story. It was about this young girl of twenty-five who was going to do away with herself as she was working in this brothel for ten years before she found out all the other girls were getting paid.

Oh yes, I've learned a lot from Aldenham library.

Of course, we try to keep up the good work when my son comes home at weekends. He sometimes brings home a couple of friends for Sunday lunch. Well, it's not really a meal, it's more a commando raid with knives and forks. They clear all the food off the table then they start looking at each other hungrily …

Eric's Rough Notes for
Luton Town FC Civic Hall Reception

I'M GLAD ITS MY TURN.. AS IT GIVES ME THE CHANCE TO GET THE CREASES OUT OF MY

UNDERPANTS...... MY LORDS .. IF THERE ARE ANY HER.. MR. CHAIRMAN...FELLOW

DIRECTORS ... LADIES AND GENTLEMEN... AND ANY THING ELSE THAT MAY HAVE CREPT

IN.....I HAVE BEEN ASKED TO WELCOME OUR GUESTS WHICH I DO MOST SINCERLY.

BUT I WOULD ALSO LIKE TO SAY THANK YOU TO ALL THE PEOLE WHO PAID...WE HAVE

A VERY IMMPRESIVE LIST OF GUESTS..... THE M.P. FOR LUTON... ....

OF WHOM IT HAS BEEN SAID... ALSO THE MAYOR OF LUTON..................

OF WHOM IT CANT BE SAID.. MR.................... OF WHOM IT SHOULD NEVER BE

SAID. BECAUSE NONE OF US HERE HAVE THE NERVE..

AND A SPECIAL WELCOME TO THE SPEAKER OF THE HOUSE..... MY WIFE OF WHOM EVERY

THINGS BEEN SAID....XXXXXXXXXXXXXXXXXXXXXXXXXXXXXXXXXXXXXXXXXXXXXXXXXXXX

XXXXXXXXXXXXXXXXXX..... IT GIVES ME GREAT PLEASURE LADIES AND GENTLEMEN BUTI

SHOULDNT BE TELLING YOU ABOUT MY PRIVATE LIFE....MAY I SAY CONGATULATIONS TO

LUTON TOWN FOOBALL CLUB ON THEIR WONDER FUL ATCHEIVMENT THIS YEAR.. THIS IS

XXXX IN MY OPINION ALL DUE TO THE EFFORT AND GEN... OF ONE MAN AND ONE MAN ALOI

THIS MAN HAS MADE THE CLUB WHAT IT IS TODAY... BUT I DONT WANT TALK ABOUT MY SI

SELF... LUTON F. C . HAVE MANY PEOPLE TO THANK AND ONE CANT MENTOIN THEM ALL

AS THERE ARE SO MANY... I WAS VERY SUPRISED TO FIND OUT HOW MANY PEOPLE WORK

FOR LUTON TOWN F. C. ... ABOUT HALF OF THEM.... I'M OFTEN ASKED IF I KNOW

ANY GOOD FOOTBALL STORIES.. WELL I DONT...BUT I DO KNOW OF AN INCIDENT

THAT HAPPENEND TO ALEC STOCK.. A FEW WEEKS AGO HE WENT TO A BARBERS IN LUTON

AND THE BARBER SAID WOULD YOU LIKE ANYTHING OFF THE TOP... AND ALEC SAID YES

THE OREINT...... AND BY THE WAY.. I HOPE YOU HAVE ALL ENJOYED THE MEAL...

YOU DONT KNOW THIS BUT YOU'VE JUST EATEN THE REFEREE WHO DISALOWED THAT GOAL

WE SCORED AGINST ....YOU CAN HARDLY CALL BEING A PROFESSIONAL FOOTBALLER

A SECURE JOB.. LOOK AT TONY HATELY.. HE'S ON THE MOVE AGAIN... HE'S HAD MORE

CLUBS THAN TONY JACKLIN...I QUITE HONESTLY SAY WHEN I WAS MADE A DIRECTOR OF

2

LUTON TOWN IT WAS ONE OF THE PROUDEST MOMENTS OF MY LIFE...I WAS REALLY
DELIGHTED TO BE MADE A DIERECTOTPR OF LUTON.. BECAUSE I LOVE COMEDY...AND
YOU WOULD'NT BELIEVE THE HARD WORK THAT TAKES PLACE WHEN WE HOLD A DIRECTORS
MEETING. AT OUR LAST MEETING THE CHAIRMAN SAID TO US... LADS? KEEP THIS UP
AND WE'LL HAVE ENOUGH MONEY BACK OFF THE EMPTIES TO BUY BOBBY MORE.....
A GOOD SPEECH AS FAR AS I'M CONCERNED IS A SHORT ONE AND WHEN I SAYAA SHORT
ONE I THINK OF ERNIE.... I KNOW WHAT YOU THOUGHT WHEN I STOOD UP. YOU THOUGHT
HE LOOKS TALLER ON T. V. ERNIE MUST BE SMALL.. LADIES AND GENTLEMEN... ERN. IS
SHORT AS A MATTER OF FACT ERN IS SO SMALL..THAT HE IS HERE TO NIGHT AND WE
HAVE'NT FOUND HIM YET.. ... I'M HAVING A GREAT TIME THIS EVENING..AAND
THIS PLACE THE CIVIV HALL IS A BEAUTIFUL PLEGE... THE MANAGER TOLD ME THAT
THIS YEAR ALONE THEY HAVE SPENT 2.. 15...0.... ON REDECORATIONS ALONE...THEY'VE
PUT A DOOR ON THE LADIES AND THATS SPIOLT MY EVENING FOR A START...HX HOW
EVER I HAVEXA DUTY TO DO SO LADIES AND GENTLEMEN IF YOU WOULD RISE AND BE
UPSTANDING.... WHILE I SIT DOWN MY LEGS ARE KILLING ME... THANK YOU...

Acknowledgements

A book of this nature is always dependent on the generous cooperation of others. My profound thanks, therefore, to all my father's peers from Lancashire who so kindly allowed me to impose during my research into his early years.

Also, my thanks to those of stage, screen and television who, likewise, squeezed me into their hectic schedules to make enlightening observations for this book. I can honestly say that all those who have contributed have given me a fuller picture of my own father, for the first time in my life.

Thanks to Natalie and Daniel and all at HarperCollins for their continued support and friendship; and to my literary agent Jennifer Luithlen for advising me so wisely over countless years. And to Suzanne Westrip at Billy Marsh Associates, who does such a remarkable job representing the estates of Morecambe and Wise.

Finally, thanks to my friends and family, who no doubt regard my obsession with M&W as … well – an obsession! Yet still they stick by me!

Absolutely finally, to Eric and Ernie themselves, who brought us the sunshine in which I've occasionally been able to bathe. And my thanks to my sister, Gail, for coming up with Eric's own words for the title of this book.

ERIC: *You had a phone call while you were out. Alfred someone!*
ERNIE: *[Excited] HITCHCOCK!*
ERIC: *He might have, I didn't ask …*

There's no answer to that …!

Sources

Bring Me Sunshine, Eric Morecambe and Ernie Wise (Futura, 1979)

Funny Man, Gary Morecambe (Methuen, 1982)

Funny Way to be a Hero, John Fisher (Paladin, 1976)

Hello, I Must Be Going: Groucho and His Friends, Charlotte Chandler (Robson, 1979)

Morecambe and Wife, Joan Morecambe (Pelham, 1985)

Parkinson, Michael Parkinson (Elm Tree Books, 1975)

Still On My Way to Hollywood, Ernie Wise (Duckworth, 1990)

The Media Mob, Barry Fantoni and George Melly (Collins, 1980)

Internet: www.ericandern.co.uk

Index